Principles of Marketing

Principles of Export Guidebooks

Series Editor: Michael Z. Brooke

Principles of Marketing Ken Wainwright
Principles of Law Relating to Overseas Trade Nicholas Kouladis
Principles of International Trade and Payments Peter Briggs
Principles of International Physical Distribution Jim Sherlock
Principles of International Marketing Julia Spencer
Principles of International Marketing Research L.W.J. Groves
Principles of Management in Export James Conlan

Principles of Marketing

Ken Wainwright

First published 1994

Blackwell Publishers
108 Cowley Road
Oxford OX4 1JF
UK

238 Main Street
Cambridge, Massachusetts 02142
USA

British Library Cataloguing in Publication Data

A CIP catalogue record for this book is available from the British Library.

Library of Congress Cataloging-in-Publication Data

A CIP catalog record for this book is available from the Library of Congress.

ISBN 0-631-19164-X

Typeset in 11½pt on 13½pt Garamond Light by Aitch Em Wordservice, Aylesbury, Buckinghamshire, Great Britain.

Printed in Great Britain by Hartnolls Limited, Bodmin, Cornwall.

This book is printed on acid-free paper.

Contents

Foreword   **ix**

Series Editor's Introduction   **xi**

About The Institute of Export Examinations   **xiii**

List of Abbreviations   **xvii**

1   The Marketing Concept   **1**
The Marketing Process   1
Responsibilities of the Marketing Manager   4
Channels of Distribution   6
Product Mix   8
The Marketing Plan   11
The Marketing Mix   12
Questions for Discussion   14

2   Market Research   **17**
Objectives of Market Research   17
Consumer Research   20
Industrial Market Research   22
Secondary Data   23
Primary Data   25
Market Selection   29
Omnibus Surveys   30

Sources of Information 31
Questions for Discussion 31

3 Product Development **33**
Range of Products 33
Models and Sizes 34
Product Life Cycle 35
Total Product Concept 39
Needs of Different Markets 40
Packing for Export 42
Questions for Discussion 46

4 Promotion **47**
Consumer Goods 47
Industrial Products 48
Public Relations 49
Sales Literature 51
Direct Mail 52
Merchandising Displays 53
Trade Fairs 54
Promotional Films 57
Visits to Customers 58
Sponsorship 59
Questions for Discussion 60

5 Pricing **61**
Direct Production Costs 61
Promotion Costs 62
Distribution Costs 63
Competitors' Prices 65
Cost of Packing 66
State of Demand 67
Profit Margins 68
Credit Risks 68
Agents' Commission 70
Questions for Discussion 71

6 Selling **73**
Sales Forecasts 73

Selling Expenses 74
Quoting in a Foreign Currency 75
Export Quotation Terms 75
Types of Sales Organization 76
Recruitment, Training and the Management
of Sales Staff 84
Export of Capital Equipment 85
Selection of an Overseas Agent 86
Agreement for an Overseas Commission Agent 88
Specimen Agreements 92
Questions for Discussion 103

7 Communication **105**
Internal Communication 105
Advertising 106
Working with Own Sales Staff 109
Working with United Kingdom based
Advertising Agencies 111
Working with an Overseas Advertising Agency 112
The Importance of Foreign Language Material 113
Questions for Discussion 114

8 Political and Legal Constraints **115**
Economic, Political and Legal Constraints 115
Packing Regulations 118
Import Duties and Quotas 120
Import Licences 121
Product Modification 123
Non-tariff Barriers 127
Questions for Discussion 129

9 The Needs of Regulatory Bodies **131**
National Standards 131
Marketing Knowhow 136
Licensing 137
Franchising 143
Questions for Discussion 145

10 United Kingdom Marketing and Exporting:
Similarities and Differences   147
  Similarities: Marketing strategy   147
                       Market selection   148
                       Decision making   149
                       Sales personnel   151
  Differences: Cultural and economic   152
                       Languages   153
                       Legal issues   154
                       Political stability   156
                       Documentation   157
                       Finance   159
                       Overseas sales personnel   160
                     ✗ Market segmentation   160
                       Overseas market research   161
  Problems for the First time Exporter   162
  Agency Agreements   163
  Questions for Discussion   164

11 Marketing in Practice   165
  The Decision to Export   165
  International Distribution   166
  Creating a Marketing and Sales Plan   168
  Overseas Marketing Channels   170
  Market Penetration   172
  Export Correspondence   173
  Barriers to International Trade   175
  Internationalization   175
  Questions for Discussion   180

Recommended Reading   181
  Other Publications   181
  Other Sources of Information   182

Glossary   183

Index   184

Foreword

It is a privilege to welcome this, the first of a new series of books especially designed for export education, the need for which is recognized ever more clearly these days.

It is also a pleasure in that the author of this introduction to export marketing is Ken Wainwright who, after a career as an exporter, built up an outstanding reputation as an export educator when he established an Institute recognised post-graduate course at the Buckinghamshire College of Higher Education which marked such a notable advance in the available expertise. He has served The Institute in many other capacities, including a period as a Member of Council.

This short and readable book is destined to spread this expertise amongst The Institute's students and members, as well as to general readers anxious to improve their performance as exporters. The author has usefully directed attention also to other forms of help that are available.

The Earl of Limerick, President,
The Institute of Export

Series Editor's Introduction

In launching the first of this series of guidebooks to the profession of exporting, the series editor – along with others associated with the project – is especially pleased that the famous Ken Wainwright is the author.

This book was easily the first to be completed because the material was all there in the author's memory, drawing on long years of experience. He also refers to the help provided by government departments. The successful exporter contacts the Department of Trade and Industry, the Foreign Office and (let it be said) the British Council to find his or her way around commercial markets in various parts of the world. He receives marvellous service, as the author says, from all these departments but some of the services described may have been modified for reasons of economy by the time you read this book.

There is another book in this series which approaches marketing in a different way, but all the books are preoccupied with bringing products to foreign markets (what else is export about?) and this series-starter – which reviews the whole subject – sets the scene which all our authors will be following as they colour in their parts of the plan.

May I welcome you, the reader, and hope to meet you again as the other books in the series appear on all aspects of export which you need to know: law (for the non-lawyer), transport and distribution, international marketing, market research and export management.

The main focus of Ken's book is on the market itself – how to investigate and adapt to it. Adapting is half the battle.

Michael Z. Brooke

About The Institute of Export Examinations

The Institute is grateful for the initiative of Michael Z. Brooke, the series editor, and Blackwell Publishers in publishing this unique series of books specially written for the Professional Examinations.

The authors for the series have been carefully selected and have specialized knowledge of their subjects, all being established lecturers or examiners for the Professional Examinations.

The books have been written in a style that is of benefit not only to students of The Institute but also to commercial organizations seeking further information about specific aspects of international trade.

Professionalism in export is vital for every company if they are to compete successfully in world markets and this new series of books provides a sound basis of knowledge for all those seeking a professional qualification in export through The Institute of Export's Professional Examinations.

The following are the subjects covered in the section of The Institute's syllabus for the 'Advanced Certificate in Overseas Trade' (Professional Examination Part I).

Principles of Marketing

Objectives of the Syllabus

1 To provide an understanding of marketing in theory and

practice as a basis for education in export marketing.

2 To enable students to grasp the nature of the main areas of marketing principles, i.e., market research, selection, product development, distribution, promotion, pricing and selling methods.

3 To show the constraints, e.g., economic, political, legal, etc., within which marketing operates.

4 To examine the differences between planning for home and international marketing.

The marketing concept

The development, promotion and distribution of products and services to satisfy the needs of industry and the consumer – the wholesale and retail trade – at a profit.

Marketing in practice

The investigation of markets abroad to determine customer requirements.

The development of a marketing plan to decide how these can be met. The plan will cover the marketing policies of the firm; the mix of products and services to be provided; the way customers are to be informed about these; how they are to be made available and sold (directly or through distributors); the investment and personnel required; and the profitability of these operations.

Marketing procedures

To carry out the marketing plan, certain specific activities are required:

1 *Market research (consumer and industrial)* A range of techniques is available (these are covered in more detail in Part II: Export Markets) to measure the nature of the market, e.g., who will buy the product; how, when and where and at what price they will buy it; what are the factors in their

buying decisions. Research is also needed into the structure of the market, e.g., who are our competitors and how do their products, distribution systems, services and marketing promotions compare with ours.

2 *Product Development* The information obtained through market research will be used to decide what sort of product or service is required, of what quality and performance, in what range of variety, models, sizes, etc., what services are required in association with it, e.g., delivery, instructions for use, spares and repairs.

The exporting firm usually needs to sell in more than one market and must decide, for example, if a single product range can be sold in several different markets; and what adaptations are required to meet various national standards or are desirable to appeal to the varying requirements of customers in these markets. Packing for international transport and branding and packaging for various markets must also be considered.

3 *Promotions* Customers need information about the firm's products and services through such media as the press and television advertising, sales literature, direct mail, trade exhibitions, sampling, merchandising displays and public relations. The firm can use an advertising agency or work in co-operation with its distributors to maximize awareness of its products and to influence customers' buying decisions.

Special factors in promotion abroad, e.g., use of foreign languages, adaptation to differences in culture and business practice, the production of company films, visits to potential customers.

4 *Pricing* Factors which enter into the price charged, i.e., production, sales and distribution costs, state of demand, competitors' prices, profit margins.

Export pricing – the need to assess how the above elements may differ in each market and also to take into account the additional cost of transport, credit risks, agents' commission and the local competitor situation. The merits of quoting in foreign currency.

5 *Selling* A factor here is the extent to which sales depend on personal selling as compared with the promotional activities

listed above. What is the nature of the sales task? Compare the differing methods and channels applied to selling to industrial users and the retail trades. The recruitment, training and management of sales staff. Setting sales targets and measuring effectiveness.

In exporting, each foreign market must be looked at separately. What do we need to do to sell in this market? Do we use our own representatives or sell there through a local agent or distributor? If the latter, how do we ensure that his sales methods are effective and that he receives the required back-up services? Which sales decisions can be taken in the market and which must be referred to UK management?

6 *Communication* No plan will work unless it lays down how it will be communicated to those who have to carry it out and how reporting will be channelled both up and down within the firm.

R.T. Ebers FIEx,
Director of Education & Training,
The Institute of Export

List of Abbreviations

Central Office of Information... COI
Department of Trade and Industry............................ DTI
Overseas Status Report Service.................................. OSRS
Overseas Promotion Support...................................... OPS
Export Credit Guarantee Department........................ ECGD
Products and Export Policy.. PEP
Classification, packaging and labelling regulations.. CPL
General Agreement on Tariffs and Trade.................. GATT
Technical Help for Exporters...................................... THE
British Standards Institution...................................... BSI
International Electrotechnical Commission............... IEC
American National Standards Institute....................... ANSI
Federal Communications Commission....................... FCC
Food and Drug Administration.................................. FDA
Canadian Standards Association................................ CSA
International News on Standards and Exporting..... *INSTEP*
Export Marketing Research Scheme.......................... EMRS
Market Information Enquiry Service.......................... MIES
British Overseas Trade Board..................................... BOTB

Terms of Delivery

Free on Board.. FOB
Cost, insurance and freight... CIF

Ex works .... EXW
Free carrier .... FCA
Free alongside ship .... FAS
Cost and freight .... CFR
Carriage paid to .... CPT
Carriage and insurance paid to .... CIP
Delivered at frontier .... DAF
Delivered ex ship .... DES
Delivered ex quay .... DEQ
Delivered duty unpaid .... DDU
Delivered duty paid .... DDP

1

The Marketing Concept

The marketing concept is the development, promotion and distribution of products and services to satisfy the needs of industry and commerce, both wholesale and retail, at a profit. The various principles of marketing are all closely related and, indeed, interdependent. Hence the individual components should not be considered in isolation but as integral parts of the overall marketing concept. This book attempts to provide a comprehensive understanding not only of marketing theories but, above all, of the application of these theories in practice when engaged in export marketing.

The Marketing Process

Awareness of the growing role played by marketing as a result of the rapid changes which are taking place in the field of foreign trade is critical to success. In the nineteenth century, Britain established an unchallenged position as the world's major exporting country, providing roughly a third of the world's total exports. A major contributory factor was the existence of the Empire which provided an enormous market and was, in effect, largely an extension of the home market; the Empire created a ready made range of export opportunities. Since World War II the whole pattern of overseas trade has changed, not only with the replacement of the Empire by the

Commonwealth, but especially by the emergence of many other major exporting nations such as the United States, Germany and Japan. These countries have gained a substantial stake in world trade, largely due to pursuing relentlessly well-organized marketing campaigns. Every year, many other countries are emerging as serious competitors in the field of foreign trade.

In the past some companies looked upon exporting as an outlet for the disposal of surplus, or possibly obsolete, production. These days have long since gone and, to succeed in the export field, an organization must be prepared to devise a clearly defined marketing strategy; this involves the investment of time, finance and personnel. All too often the term marketing is thought of as another name for selling, and it should be emphasized that the marketing function embraces responsibility for a wide range of activities – in addition to selling – such as research, design, production, development, finance, advertising, promotion, and where appropriate, after sales service.

Each of these functions is an integral part of the marketing process. The concept of marketing is not to focus on the product, but to focus on the customer and, by integrated marketing, to achieve profits. Detailed below are some of the major functions of marketing.

1 *Product innovation* To help with product innovation and development, to review, research and revise products in accordance with customers' needs.
2 *Product range* To ensure that the product range is stabilized and streamlined, and that uneconomic lines are eliminated.
3 *Production* To ensure that production, and with it employment are maintained at the optimum level.
4 *Marketing efficiency and service* To maintain the marketing organization at a high level of efficiency, controlling the sales effort and ensuring a high degree of service to customers.
5 *Costing and planning* To cooperate with management in costing and planning.
6 *Coordination* To cooperate with other departments in the company and keep all sections informed of progress and any changes.

7 *Physical distribution* To ensure that the physical distribution of goods meets the needs of company policy.

8 *Profit* To ensure that all operations contribute to optimum profit, survival, and growth of the company.

A vital element in the marketing process is the creation of good relationships with customers, comprising not only the people or organizations that will use the goods or services, but also the distributors and agents who form an integral part of the chain of distribution.

In the past, some companies tended to concentrate their efforts on devising and producing products or services and then made efforts to find suitable outlets overseas. A more realistic approach to marketing is to focus not on the product but on the customer and to achieve profits by integrated marketing. Thus marketing becomes the very reason for a company's existence. It is of vital importance to everyone within a company, from designers to technicians and production departments, indeed all company personnel who should be aware of the marketing aims of the company and think of the satisfaction of their customers' needs at a profit as the most important factor in their day to day operations.

A company adopts the marketing concept by gearing all its activities to satisfying customer needs. Whereas, in the past, many companies directed their efforts solely to increasing production of products which could then be sold to their customers by hard selling and promotion, a marketing oriented company will be more concerned with obtaining profits through achieving the maximum level of customer satisfaction.

Accepting the general principle of aiming to achieve customer satisfaction, thought must be given to what a customer may expect from an exporter. First and foremost the customer will seek a product or service which is totally acceptable in terms of quality, durability, performance and price. In addition it is extremely important to make the product available at the right place and time by ensuring that steps are taken to organize suitable distribution and delivery arrangements.

Consideration must also be given to satisfying the needs of wholesalers and retailers which form an important link between the exporter and the final customer. Attention must be paid to such factors as discounts, trade margins and credit policies to ensure an adequate return for their contribution to the marketing chain.

In the same way, the organizations in the distribution chain together with the ultimate customer must be able to rely on the maintenance of delivery promises and quality standards.

Further examples of factors which must be considered as part of the general marketing process will be: the provision of advertising support; assistance with trade exhibitions; and the provision of sales promotion material and point of sale display aids. In the case of certain products another vital consideration will be the provision of efficient after sales service facilities.

In order to maximize revenue from sales, it is a duty of the marketing function to consider a variety of costs in addition to the costs of developing and producing its products. For example, such recent and far reaching developments as containerization, palletization, roll-on/roll-off services and the concept of unit loads provide excellent opportunities for an exporter to achieve significant savings in transport and distribution costs.

Responsibilities of the Marketing Manager

The responsibilities of the marketing manager are considerable and varied. Bearing in mind the decision of a marketing oriented company to strive to satisfy its customers' needs at a profit, it has a prime responsibility to maintain the closest possible contact with customers and achieve a clear understanding of a customer's needs and objectives. This will be achieved by maintaining the closest possible contact with customers and by understanding market research and technical research. These functions will be discussed in detail in the following chapter.

A most important element of a marketing manager's function is to maintain close contact with all departments in the company to ensure that they are fully aware of the objectives which the company wishes to achieve. Initially, close contact must be maintained with the research and development department in order to help with product innovation and development and to ensure that every effort in this department is directed towards satisfying customer needs.

The product range has to be kept under constant review. As new items are introduced to meet the demands of customers, it will almost certainly be necessary to eliminate some older lines from the product range.

The marketing manager must be in constant liaison with the production departments to achieve a balance between what can be produced and what customers need with the objective of maintaining the highest possible levels of production and employment.

An essential element of the marketing manager's responsibilities is to maintain the closest possible liaison with management in order to play an ongoing role in arriving at appropriate decisions on costing and pricing.

Additionally, the marketing manager needs to cooperate closely with all the other departments to ensure that they are fully informed of progress and changes in plans.

A further duty is to monitor and control every aspect of the physical distribution of a company's products.

The marketing manager's overriding responsibility is to ensure that all the company's activities contribute to achieving the company's aims at a profit.

Successful marketing management can well be illustrated by describing a true marketing success story. The family owned company, Baxter's of Speyside started life as a small grocery shop in 1868. In 1914 the founder's son opened a small plant devoted to producing the popular products of his jam-making wife. As late as 1950 sales were a mere £40,000 and Baxter's only had 11 employees. Today the company is the premier producer of quality soups in Europe (probably in the world), employs over 650 people and is recognized as a major purveyor of fine foods; it has an annual turnover of some £35m and profits of £3.5m. The product range has grown over the years to a total of some 450 lines which are marketed in about 60 countries worldwide.

Essentially, Baxter's growth and success is based on a range of popular products, essential prerequisites for a successful marketing operation.

In the late 1940s, post war government policies allowed makers of jams one extra ton of sugar if the jam was for export. The instant reaction of Baxter's was for their Chairman to make an exploratory visit to the United States to investigate the possibility of meeting the needs of that market. On his return he stated that he discovered what was to him a new word – 'marketing' – a word which, he claimed, was invented by a Scottish professor at Harvard. He also stated that, after this initial visit to the United States, the company 'no longer simply made good things and hoped to sell them, we found out what the market wanted first'. This statement expresses admirably what marketing really means. It is significant that Baxter's are now the largest exporters of soup into the United States.

Having started as a small manufacturer, with a limited range of jams and soups, a wide range of more exotic lines has been produced over the years in response to customer demand. The business is run with set targets and any product which fails to achieve the sales target is discontinued. An important element of the marketing programme is to monitor and meet a wide range of international food fads. The company admits, for example, 'We make a soup for Japan that you just wouldn't eat in this country'.

Channels of Distribution

Channels of distribution vary according to the type of product as well as the target market.

Below are some factors to be taken into consideration when selecting channels of distribution.

1 In the case of perishable products, a major consideration will be delivery time and the speediest channels.
2 If a product is branded or packaged for distribution to a wide range of outlets, selection of wholesalers or multiples is important.

3 Products with a high unit value will frequently be sold direct to appropriate retail outlets.
4 In the case of specialized capital equipment, this will usually be sold direct to the end user.
5 Bulky products will frequently be sold to a distributor or wholesaler which possesses appropriate storage facilities and an organization for onward distribution.
6 In the case of items with a high rate of turnover it will be important to consider distribution through either wholesalers or retail multiples offering suitable warehouse facilities.
7 Another important factor is that the chosen outlet must be appropriate for the image of the product, for example: specialist retailers for items such as perfumery, jewellery, china, glass and quality furniture. The outlets will vary from country to country and the exporter always needs to check.

In addition to these channels of distribution which are concerned with direct contact with the overseas customers, it may be appropriate in certain instances to deal with one of the various United Kingdom based intermediaries mentioned below.

For the newcomer to exporting, a simple way to tackle initial export orders would be by using the services of an Export House. An Export House frequently represents a buyer overseas, confirming orders on behalf of the overseas buyer and taking responsibility for payment and shipment. In many cases an Export House will specialize in a particular range of products.

A further possibility would be to make sales through an export merchant. Such a merchant acts as a principal, buying from the manufacturer at ex-works or Free on Board (FOB) prices. He then arranges shipment and payment by the overseas customer, making the transaction for the manufacturer like a home market sale.

Although the above mentioned marketing channels may prove attractive to a manufacturer who lacks the organization, skills and staff to undertake direct exporting, they do have a major disadvantage in that they deprive the manufacturer of the all important direct contact with the customer overseas.

A further variation on this theme is dealing through export buying houses. A growing number of overseas buyers, especially retail stores, tend to establish their own buying offices in the United Kingdom responsible for organizing purchases either in the United Kingdom or sometimes throughout Europe. In addition, some overseas governments have established buying offices in the United Kingdom. For the exporter such buying houses provide an opportunity of obtaining export business without leaving the United Kingdom and the buying office provides not only a direct link with the overseas customer but also a way for the exporter to avoid credit risks, obtain payment in the United Kingdom and carry out overseas business without establishing a number of overseas accounts.

In recent years there has been an important newcomer in the field of marketing – the factor. Basically, factoring is a financial operation which has been in operation for many years in the United States. For a fee the factor will undertake the function of sales accounting and collection, offering complete protection against credit risk, and if required will provide immediate payment at the time of invoicing the customer. One of the benefits which the service offers to the exporter is that it reduces the exporter's sales ledger to a single account – the factor. The exporter is thereby relieved of the need to provide staff to produce statements and send reminders to customers. It is the factor who takes on board the task of collecting payment from the overseas buyer, together with the corresponding credit risk.

Some factors operating internationally will offer in addition to the basic financial operation, such services as packing, forwarding, shipping and insurance, a specific quotation being provided by the factor in accordance with the services required.

Product Mix

In a number of industries – especially the manufacture of consumer goods – customers frequently expect to see the introduction of new lines every year. Obviously this situation arises in the case of goods which have a purely seasonal appeal. In order to satisfy customers' demands the manufacturer will naturally tend to offer new lines. With the addition of new lines to the product range, the manufacturer must make a frequent evaluation of the range of products on offer, and discontinue some of the older less popular lines to keep the product mix within reasonable limits.

In a number of export markets, especially where there is strong competition, it may be wise to make a survey of the level of demand for all the products available and then select a limited range to be offered in each market. In order to sustain a maximum level of profitability the exporter should aim to offer a limited range of high volume sales lines. In addition to new products there will always be the problem of modifying or up-grading some existing lines. Such new lines or modified existing lines must be related to the company's plans for an adequate return on investment. The anticipated revenues from existing products and markets must be related to the projected growth of sales and profits. Especially in overseas markets every effort will be made to limit the number of products which only have seasonal demand. Where a company has a poor product mix, this will not only jeopardize sales but may well create problems due to unused production facilities. There may be a situation where a disproportionate amount of profits comes from a limited number of products, therefore sales and profits could decline and indeed it may not be possible to utilize fully the efforts of the sales force.

It is important to consider the consistency of the product mix. For example, how closely are products related in terms of end-use, production facilities and distribution channels?

There are a number of ways in which the best possible use may be made of a product mix. It may be possible to increase sales in existing overseas markets, or to seek new markets as additional outlets for existing products. Alternatively, it may be possible to create new products for existing markets or introduce new products for a range of new markets.

Great care is required when considering an increase in the product mix. It will be of prime importance to consider if proposed new products can be produced with existing production facilities and labour. The answer to these questions will reflect the possible need for new plant or additional labour. Should such additional facilities be needed, it will be necessary to evaluate the potential demand for the proposed product, in order to make a considered judgement on the advisability of making any addition to the product range.

With a variety of possible new products, other matters must be considered. For example, will the existing sales force be able to handle the product, or will retraining be necessary? In addition, consideration must be given to the ability of existing agents or distributors to handle the proposed additions to the product range.

If production facilities are available and it is felt that the existing sales staff could handle additional new lines, the next stage would be to consider the potential markets for the product, either existing or new markets. It will be essential to undertake market research and consider market reports in order to determine if, in fact, a market exists for the product which will produce adequate levels of sales and an acceptable return on investment in the new product.

The average failure rate for new products is normally very high and in view of the additional costs involved in introducing a new product in an overseas market it is essential that any proposed addition to the product range should be carefully researched before any final decisions are taken.

A very important aspect of any proposal to extend a product range is to determine which existing products may have to be eliminated. Older products for which sales are declining incur a wide range of unnecessary costs. They may, for example, involve short production runs, require price and stock adjustment and take up a disproportionate amount of management time. Inevitably agents or distributors will tend to concentrate their best efforts on newer lines for which there is a ready market demand. If a decision is made to eliminate a product, a number of options are available.

Perhaps it may be decided to eliminate the product without delay. However, consideration must be given to the possibility that if customers decide to replace the product with alternatives from your competitors, they may also decide to transfer some of their other business to your competitors. An alternative would be to increase the price and allow demand to fall away. This option would have the benefit of producing a better profit margin during the remaining life of the product.

There are, however, some examples of situations where it may be good commercial sense to retain older less popular items in production. This would apply, for example, in the case of china and earthenware tableware. In this industry companies may guarantee to keep certain patterns in production for a specified number of years. This will be an incentive to customers to buy the product, and even as sales decline, the manufacturer will reap much goodwill from their customers, who will have a strong incentive to make future new purchases from the same manufacturer. In fact, such an arrangement could well prove to be an excellent low cost, long term public relations exercise.

The Marketing Plan

A most important part of successful marketing is a well constructed marketing plan which outlines objectives, and explains how they will be achieved. The marketing plan must have the full support of all involved in its execution. Composition and emphasis will vary with each individual company.

In drawing up a marketing plan, the first essential is to establish the present and potential size of the market, and then to establish a range of specific objectives, either by country, region or commodity. It will be necessary to establish the degree and type of competition in the market, together with an analysis of prevailing price levels. Having reached this point the next step will be to establish a budget for sales income by country, region or commodity. It is also important to set an achievable time scale, allowing sufficient lead time to enable the targets to be achieved.

The marketing plan must take into consideration the available selling resources and ensure that sufficient staff and resources will be available to achieve the targets set. Consideration must be given to the degree of promotion and advertising which will be necessary. In order to promote the product a variety of aids need to be considered.

In addition to catalogues, brochures and press, television and trade fairs may be considered appropriate. However, in addition to the needs of different products, a major factor will be the cost and the overall income potential.

When drawing up a marketing plan for an overseas market it will be necessary to look closely at problems of distribution and, depending on the facilities available, within the company; it may be wise to consider enlisting the help of a freight forwarder.

Further factors which must be investigated and considered will be the existence of any tariff or non-tariff barriers which could have an impact on any proposed marketing plan. Also important are credit control arrangements to ensure that payment is received on the date due.

It is obvious that marketing objectives will only be achievable with the help of an efficient distribution system. In view of the varied information which must be obtained to construct an effective marketing plan it will be obvious that at a very early stage a market research programme must be undertaken. Initially this may be home based research, making use of some of the information available within one's own company – especially an analysis of company records including sales by products and sales by territories. Further factors which must be considered will be the number of new products available, general sales trends over previous years, current sales, size of markets, general trading conditions and the future economic outlook. Having exhausted the existing information available within the company full use should be made of the wide range of external sources of information which are available. These are covered in detail in chapter 2. When preliminary plans have been suggested, it will be important to consider the potential profit contribution of various products. Of equal importance will be the need to have an up-to-date forecast of the company's production capacity. Finally careful consideration must be given to any marketing expenses which will be involved.

The Marketing Mix

The marketing mix is commonly referred to as the 4 Ps – Product, Price, Place and Promotion. The ingredients of the mix will be selected from the following: the product, packing, price, the selling function, methods of distribution, sales promotion, advertising and publicity, market research and public relations. A satisfactory marketing mix for a product will be achieved by taking all these factors into consideration and the final choice will be made from the findings of market research which will indicate an appropriate marketing mix to meet a specific situation.

Market research must be undertaken to determine the acceptability of a product in a particular market. It must be remembered that it is essential to tailor a product to meet the needs of customers in a particular market as success will depend heavily on offering a good product, appropriate to the needs of each individual market.

Depending on the type of product, attention must be given to ensuring that both the immediate packaging, which may prove to be a valuable promotion tool, is appropriate together with the final packing which must be acceptable for the chosen market.

Obviously, a very important aspect of the marketing mix will be the price. In arriving at a price a number of factors must be taken into consideration. First and foremost the price must provide an adequate return for the exporter, and must be competitive and attractive to the customer.

Selling methods and channels of distribution have to be considered carefully and adjusted to meet the needs of each individual market. It would, for example, be inappropriate to tell a customer that a particular method was acceptable in the United States. The customer company will rightly seek selling methods and channels of distribution which are tailored to meet the needs of its particular market and which may well differ from those which are acceptable in the United States.

It must be remembered that methods of sales promotion have to be devised for each individual market, bearing in mind the restrictions which are frequently imposed on various types of sales promotion.

As will be appreciated, the marketing mix has to be tailored to the needs of each market. This will be particularly necessary in the field of advertising. Here, as in the case of sales promotion, many markets have clearly defined rules which must be observed. In addition it is important to make a detailed analysis of the advertising opportunities which may be available.

For example, in certain markets some vehicles for advertising, which are accepted as normal in the United Kingdom (such as national newspapers and television), may not be available.

In many markets it will be essential to consider trade fairs and exhibitions as important possibilities for publicity and advertising. A further important factor will be the possible benefits to be obtained from public relations. Here again the type of public relations exercise which will be the most rewarding will vary from market to market.

A successful marketing operation will be based on the coordination of the variables already referred to and it is important to appreciate that the final marketing mix selected may well vary in each individual market. Existing literature provides countless examples of the adjustments which were necessary to fit products or services to meet the needs of different markets. As obvious examples differences will arise due to climatic and geographical factors, languages, cultural taboos, electricity supplies, and health and safety standards. It is most important that research be undertaken to investigate the many factors which could have an influence on the marketing mix to be chosen.

At this stage it is also necessary to be aware of the vital role that the selection of an appropriate marketing mix plays in the construction of a successful marketing programme. In later chapters, the individual components of the marketing mix will be described in detail.

It is hoped that this book will provide a detailed explanation of the material covered in the Principles of Marketing syllabus, for the professional part I examination of the Institute of Export, together with some examples of companies who have been successful in the field of marketing. The syllabus was drawn up with a view to providing sufficient preliminary training in export marketing and provides guidance for anyone interested in the subject.

Questions for Discussion

1 What do you understand by the marketing concept?

2 What are the elements which must be considered in the marketing mix?

3 Describe any five factors which must be taken into consideration when selecting channels of distribution.

2

Market Research

As competition increases everywhere, it is vital that before attempting to enter any export market comprehensive market research is undertaken.

Objectives of Market Research

Companies find it unwise to embark on the development of a new market overseas without first undertaking a comprehensive survey of the market. With the costs of launching a product overseas so high, it is essential to produce the most effective possible marketing and sales plan based on market research findings. In addition to the obvious need to ensure that the product is suitable for the market, it is also important to discover the most effective distribution system, and where appropriate to provide an after sales service. It is also important to decide upon the most effective method of advertising through analysis of the results of various media such as television, national press, radio, mail shots and others. An effective market research programme is essential to avoid hit and miss marketing and management techniques.

Initially it is important to understand what is meant by market research. It entails the gathering and interpretation of a wide range of information followed by the utilization of this information to enable reasoned conclusions to be reached.

The following are examples of the questions which may be answered by market research. Who are our competitors? How do their products, distribution systems, services and marketing promotions compare with ours?

Although a market research programme is a vital first step in any marketing project, it is important to appreciate the need for market research to be undertaken on a continuing basis. This will enable the correct management decisions to be made.

There must be quick and accurate feedback from the selected markets to enable the right decisions to be taken to produce and deliver the required products at the right time and place.

Many potential exporters fail because they do not appreciate the importance of both initial and continuing market research. To some newcomers to exporting the very mention of a market research programme conjures up visions of large-scale and expensive programmes undertaken by large companies such as the market leaders in many consumer products. Although such projects are frequently undertaken, and do involve the expenditure of much time and money, it would be wrong to overlook the more modest fields of research available to everyone.

A newcomer to exporting may believe that, because the company has for many years thrived on products which have had great success in the home or Commonwealth markets, there must necessarily be a wide range of potential export markets for its products. In the days of a flourishing Empire, many companies had a thriving export trade but this cannot be compared to the situation which exists today. When they were exporting within the Empire and enjoying the benefits of Empire preference, many of these successful exporters were really dealing with an extended home market. With the granting of independence to the colonies and the ending of Empire preference, today's exporters now face severe competition in what were previously secure markets. Remember the failure of many companies who had a thriving trade within the Empire, but failed to do their market research and adapt to a more competitive world. Information obtained from market research will help to indicate the types of products or services which are required in a market.

Failure to appreciate the changing situation has spelt disaster for many exporters. With growing competition in all markets, little success will be obtained by a potential exporter who fails to appreciate the importance of researching the needs of every market. It is vitally important to investigate each potential market to determine its precise requirements for products, prices, local regulations and existing competition.

When making a preliminary investigation of a market, it is important to establish what products are already available there, as well as what products are acceptable. An important fact to establish is not only the range of products already available from other sources but, above all, the competition from domestic producers.

A clear understanding of the major functions of market research is a must. The first fact to be established will be, quite simply, who buys what, where from and for how much. This will give the exporter an indication of the competition which exists in the market and will enable it to establish the strengths and weaknesses of its own products. It is equally important to determine if the total market for a product or service is steady, rising or falling.

Customer preferences, habits and customs need to be examined. It is also essential to determine if there are any restrictions imposed on the import of a particular product, also to determine if the product must meet any special quality, safety or health standards.

A vital factor is the public's ability to buy the product, and it is therefore important to know what price would be acceptable to the customer.

It may well be necessary to amend the product in order to make it acceptable in a market, and a detailed study of customers' needs and preferences is therefore essential.

A further aspect to be considered is that of distribution. In many markets the methods of distribution will be quite different from those which may be regarded as normal at home.

It is important to study every aspect of transporting your goods to a market, and then to make a detailed study of all the possible channels of distribution. The choice of the correct channel might have a significant effect on the successful marketing of the product.

Consumer Research

The first step in undertaking consumer research is to examine and analyse the sales records which the company may have for a market where some business has been undertaken previously and evaluate this information.

The next stage will be to investigate what other companies are achieving to establish who the potential customers are, what they buy, at what price and in what quantities. It is also important to establish exactly which products are acceptable in a given market.

The initial research will derive from the exporter's previous experience in the market, if any. Consumer research will investigate all other firms operating in a given market. This information can sometimes be obtained from published data, or possibly from overseas agents; alternatively it may be necessary to undertake a specific market research exercise in a market, using either one's own staff or a professional market research organization.

It is possible that a professional market research programme may be beyond the resources available to many smaller companies or to newcomers to exporting; it may well be necessary to commence with a small-scale operation using one's own resources.

As much of the research must be undertaken in the overseas market, it may be worth considering participation in an overseas trade fair for which a measure of assistance is usually available from the Department of Trade and Industry (DTI).

An essential element of successful market research is the correct interpretation of all information which is obtained. This point may be illustrated by recounting the experiences of two salesmen for footwear, both of whom were making their first visit to an African market. The first salesman's report was: 'There is no market here, no one wears shoes.' However, the second salesman's interpretation of the situation was totally different: 'Fantastic market potential, everyone needs shoes.'

The DTI has set up the Export Marketing Research Scheme (EMRS) to provide assistance for potential exporters. The objective of this scheme is to encourage and assist both individual companies and trade associations to undertake market research overseas as an essential first step in their export efforts. This scheme is designed specifically to assist companies who may be new to exporting or to export marketing research. Full details of the scheme appear in the range of excellent brochures which are available from the DTI.

An additional valuable source of information is the Market Information Enquiry Service (MIES) operated by the DTI. When a company has identified the markets it wishes to investigate, use of the Enquiry Service can establish the prospects for the specific products or services, how to sell into the market and who should be approached.

The British Overseas Trade Board (BOTB) was set up in 1972. It advises the DTI and the Foreign and Commonwealth Office on overseas trade and export promotion.

Overseas Trade Services operated by the DTI bring together the major government departments involved in export promotion: the DTI, the Foreign and Commonwealth Office, Scottish Trade International, Welsh Office Industry Department, and the Industrial Development Board for Northern Ireland. On a worldwide basis some 2,000 staff are dedicated to providing a wide range of advice, information and assistance to United Kingdom exporters, covering virtually every aspect of overseas marketing and enabling the potential exporter to have access to information on every aspect of export marketing such as products, importers, agents, size of markets, tariffs, import regulations, trade fairs, statistics and currencies.

Much valuable information is also available from trade associations and chambers of commerce, many of whom have built up a comprehensive range of information about overseas markets. It is likely that your own trade association and Chamber of Commerce will prove to be a valuable source of market information, directly tailored to meet the special needs of your own industry.

Another important aspect of market research is product research which is a development of normal consumer research. A number of factors must be determined about the product. First and foremost it is important to establish that a product really does the job that is claimed for it. In addition it is important to ensure that the product meets any national standards imposed in the overseas market and to investigate the potential customers' acceptance of the product.

The results of such investigations will determine if there is any need to modify the design of the product, packaging or presentation.

It is very important to understand the reasoning behind potential customers' preferences and habits. At this stage it is helpful to give examples of those products for which it will be necessary to undertake consumer research. Such research will be valuable for a wide range of fast-moving consumer goods such as foodstuffs, clothing, footwear and confectionery. Equally important is research for a number of consumer durables such as television, radio, washing machines and motor vehicles.

In addition it is becoming increasingly important to undertake consumer research in the field of services, covering for example hotels, restaurants, holidays and a range of entertainment facilities.

An example of the importance of the results obtained from this type of consumer research would be instant coffee. Many manufacturers make minor alterations to the product to meet the differing tastes in a range of markets. A further example is Guinness. This product has been introduced to an extensive range of overseas markets, but it has been necessary to make slight adjustments to both the flavour and the strength to meet the precise requirements of customers in different markets.

Industrial Market Research

In view of the enormous range of information which is available, the potential exporter's first problem will be to define precisely the information required. A vague general question can only receive a vague general answer. If the potential exporter is able to define very precisely the information which is sought, much of this will be available from the DTI.

It should, however, be appreciated that such information will require consideration and refinement to meet the detailed needs of each individual exporter.

The range of services offered by the DTI is very extensive but the following are of special interest to exporters. Export Data Services help companies to undertake preliminary desk research. The Export Market Information Centre (at Ashdown House, 123 Victoria Street, London) gives direct access to a wide range of economic statistics, trade and telephone directories and market reports as well as its own export database. In addition the DTI has available more than 600 export publications.

It will be appreciated that with industrial products it will be more difficult to obtain precise market information for specialized products than would be the case when researching markets for consumer products. In addition to the possible sources of information mentioned previously, other sources which could prove to be valuable would be trade associations, chambers of commerce and export clubs. Many of these organizations may have specific information which would be relevant for your own special industrial product.

In addition it may often be possible to acquire much valuable information by attending local meetings of The Institute of Export and The Institute of Freight Forwarders.

Many trade associations and chambers of commerce organize participation in overseas trade fairs. Such visits provide a first-class opportunity to undertake market research overseas at modest cost and these organizations can frequently provide valuable market research information relevant to your own product.

Secondary Data

Market research information falls into two distinct categories, primary and secondary.

When undertaking a market research survey of a market, it is to obtain all available secondary data. This is frequently referred to as desk research and involves an investigation and evaluation of existing information. Such information may be obtained from sources such as the DTI, chambers of commerce, trade associations, export clubs and banks. This secondary information will be general market information, provided for a variety of purposes, and will not be geared specifically to the individual needs of the exporter. Consequently, having obtained all available secondary information, it is very important that this be studied carefully in order to identify and extract any information contained in these reports which may be relevant to your own requirements.

Secondary market research information will provide an invaluable source of general market information. For example, it will give an indication of any restrictions which may be imposed in a market. Restrictions are frequently imposed to protect local industries. Where such restrictions exist, secondary market research may well reveal alternative methods of entering a market in addition to direct exports. It may, for example be worth considering the possibility of exporting components to be assembled in the market, or perhaps the manufacture of your product under licence overseas.

With many products, secondary data will indicate the existence of any special standards which must be met in a market. These standards will frequently apply in the case, for example, of foodstuffs or safety standards for a range of products especially machinery or electrical goods, boilers and pressure vessels.

At one time, British or American standards were widely accepted in overseas markets. However, as the economies of many countries have improved, there has been a growing tendency for markets to impose their own standards. It is vital to appreciate the need to meet local standards in order to enable your products to be accepted in a given market.

With the creation of a single European Market (since 31 December 1992) it is now necessary to be aware of the process of harmonization of standards in the European Community and the creation of European standards by the European Committees for Standardization (CEN, CENELEC).

In 1966 the British Standards Institution established the Technical Help for Exporters service (THE) to provide a comprehensive range of technical information for the guidance of exporters. The services provided fall into three main categories:

1 identification and provision of overseas specifications and national standards, and help in interpreting them;

2 the provision of detailed information about regulations and approval systems in overseas markets;

3 assistance to manufacturers to obtain any necessary test certificates.

As will be appreciated, the services provided by Technical Help for Exporters are invaluable to an exporter considering the export of products which may need to meet special standards prevailing in an overseas market.

Another organization which is deeply involved in export promotion is the Confederation of British Industry. A wide range of information, including publications, is available from the Confederation.

Mention has already been made of the importance of regarding market research as an ongoing process. After undertaking a market research survey, it is vital to keep up-to-date both on the situation in a given market and on market research techniques. This can be done by maintaining a constant review of articles which appear not only in the national press, but especially in *Export Today,* the official journal of The Institute of Export, and also in a range of marketing publications. Much invaluable information may be obtained from the wide range of free literature available from the DTI and the banks. In addition to general market information, the banks frequently have a range of valuable information on special markets.

Primary Data

If the results obtained from preliminary desk research are encouraging, it will be necessary to undertake field research. Information gathered by field research is known as primary data and is specifically related to the specific problems in hand.

Inevitably the acquisition of primary data is more expensive than undertaking desk research because the research must be undertaken in the foreign market.

A brief reference has already been made to the Export Marketing Research Scheme operated by the DTI. The scheme exists to help and encourage exporters to use structured export marketing research methods.

In addition to professional advice to help companies decide whether specific market research is needed, the scheme also offers financial support to companies with fewer than two hundred employees and to trade associations for approved export marketing research projects. The scheme is administered on behalf of Overseas Trade Services by the Association of British Chambers of Commerce.

When dealing with technical products, it will be advisable for the exporter to provide technical support for the research specialist who is undertaking the survey. For example, with engineering products it is vital that an engineer from the exporting company should be involved throughout, to spend time in the market investigating technical aspects with the outside consultant who will concentrate on general and commercial aspects.

Depending on the product, it may be possible to undertake market research in conjunction with an advertising agency which already has experience and contacts in an overseas market. Nevertheless, care must be taken if this option is chosen as agencies may distort their findings in order to increase the possibility of establishing justification for an advertising campaign.

Before embarking on a market research exercise, it is important to define precisely the objectives which it is hoped to achieve and to have a clear idea of the specific marketing problems to be investigated. It is also important to define the results which it is hoped to achieve. After embarking on a market research survey it is necessary to establish how it is proposed to use the research findings.

When market research is to be undertaken by an outside consultant, the scope of the scheme must be most carefully defined. For example, the markets to be studied along with the products and the market sectors must be specified.

Whichever option is chosen, the ultimate aim of the exercise will be the same. Detailed below are the basic facts to be investigated:

1 exact size of the market both in terms of value and volume;

2 segmentation of the market in terms of application, end-use sectors and geographical regions;
3 trends in 1 and 2 together with appropriate projections;
4 detailed information on import duties or quotas, technical standards and other government regulations.

On entering into an agreement with an outside consultant to undertake a market research survey the following factors need to be defined and agreed:

1 a clear definition of the products or services which the research is required to investigate;
2 a detailed list of the information required and the geographical area to be covered by the research;
3 the date by which the information is required;
4 any special areas in which detailed recommendations are required from the consultant;
5 agreement on any proposed questionnaires before field work is commenced;
6 frequency, content and location of proposed progress reports and progress meetings;
7 any special features which the exporter wishes the final report to include such as details of samples used, number of interviews, response rates, explanation of quantitative methods.

The precise nature of the final market research report will vary according to the differences in the products, markets and objectives of the survey.

It is important that the final report should follow an orderly sequence and be easy to refer to. A typical market research report would cover the following items.

Background Outlining the reasons for taking a decision to undertake the study.
Objectives A clear definition of the aims which the survey is intended to achieve.
Scope Precise details of the products and markets studied.
Methodology Details of survey methods used.
Summary of findings and conclusions Precise details of the

principal findings of the research.

Recommendations Details of what actions the exporter may be recommended to take.

Main findings A number of separate sections covering, for example, general commercial and economic background, overall market situation, geographical areas, product headings.

Appendix To provide supplementary information such as business lists, export regulations, government legislation, supporting tables of figures, specialist reviews or competitor details.

It must be remembered that consumer and industrial research involve very different techniques. Some of the major differences are outlined below.

Distribution Industrial products are usually delivered direct to customers, but consumer products usually involve various distributors and middlemen.

Products For consumer goods there is usually a quick buying cycle, and the effect of economic changes can be predicted from past experience. For industrial products, the effect of economic changes is more difficult to predict. For consumer goods there will be a relatively short manufacturing cycle, and in many cases repeat orders. Industrial products normally have a longer manufacturing cycle and are often bought on a one-off basis.

Buyer behaviour Frequently, the buyer of consumer goods may be influenced by the wishes of the final consumer who will probably lack a degree of professionalism in buying tactics. However, the buyer of industrial products will usually be highly professional and have access to expert advice.

Demand Demand for consumer goods is direct, with a multitude of buyers who will respond to price changes. In the case of industrial products, the demand is often derived. For example the demand for machinery to manufacture man-made fibres will be derived from the demand for the finished products. For industrial goods there will be fewer buyers. Demand tends to be concentrated and is inelastic due to technical considerations.

Market Selection

The results obtained from both primary and secondary research will enable decisions to be made to select markets for development.

It will obviously be impossible to export initially on a world-wide basis and it is important to select the most promising markets for your products based on the results of market research surveys.

Having made a decision about the most promising markets to be tackled, it will be necessary to consider what are the most appropriate means of entering and establishing a suitable means of permanent representation in the chosen markets. The means by which this may be achieved will be covered fully in chapter 6.

Whatever method of representation is selected, it is important to appreciate the need to establish the necessary arrangements to enable further market research to be carried out on a con-tinuous basis.

Having made an initial selection of markets which are promising, it is also important to be aware of the variety of uncontrollable circumstances which may affect marketing plans in an overseas market. The problems will vary according to the particular product and market. There will always be a danger of import restrictions being imposed to protect domestic indus-tries or local government restrictions on foreign exchange availability. For example, some market economies may depend on agricultural production which tends to vary from year to year. Alternatively, newly found natural resources may bring about a radical change in the economic situation.

The foregoing will highlight the need for international market research to continue on an ongoing basis to ensure that the exporter is always in possession of up-to-date information on each market.

There will frequently be advanced warning of changes about to take place in a market, and the exporter who is committed to undertaking constant research will be in the best possible position to react to any such warning signs, and take steps to amend marketing plans accordingly.

It should be emphasized that there are three vital factors governing market research projects. It is important that market research findings be well presented, they should also be available at frequent intervals and not only must they be studied and considered by senior management but, above all, they must be acted on.

Omnibus Surveys

Some of the ways in which it is possible to undertake market research overseas have already been identified. Researching an overseas market is likely to be both more time consuming and more costly than researching the home market. A major problem to be faced will be cultural differences. In some markets not only may interviews be difficult to obtain, but religious customs can make it impossible to interview females.

Another vital question will be the need to employ researchers with specialist language abilities.

In some countries, problems may well be created by the spread and density of the population which can create major problems for both interviewing and sampling. Although in the home market a wide range of statistical and general census information is readily available, this may not be so in many overseas markets. Whereas in the United Kingdom there are many instances where postal surveys will be valuable, this is less likely to be suitable in countries where factors such as cost, poor communications and low response rates are significant.

The interpretation of results may be suspect if the research is carried out by someone with a different cultural background from the customer to add to language difficulties. Bearing in mind the importance of market research overseas, and being aware of both the costs and possible difficulties which may be encountered, it may in some instances be wise to consider, as an initial step, taking part in an omnibus survey. Professional market research organizations have the staff and expertise to carry out market research overseas. However, for the smaller company, the cost could prove to be too much.

To overcome this problem, many market research organizations undertake omnibus surveys. These surveys cover a number of factors of interest to different exporters, and arrangements can be made for exporters to include in the survey a number of specific questions relative to their own special needs. This facility provides an opportunity for potential exporters to have the benefit of a professional market research project at the lowest possible cost.

Sources of Information

The following are the sources to which companies usually refer for information:

- Own company records
- Department of Trade and Industry
- Chambers of Commerce
- Trade associations
- Export clubs
- The Institute of Export
- The Institute of Freight Forwarders
- Technical Help for Exporters
- Confederation of British Industry
- Banks
- Export Credits Guarantee Department
- Foreign embassies
- Foreign information bureaux in the United Kingdom
- Statistics office of the European Community
- Newspapers and journals

Questions for Discussion

1 Explain what you understand by the term market research.

2 Describe the meaning of primary data and secondary data.

3 List ten possible sources of market research information.

3

Product Development

Range of Products

An important factor in determining the success or failure of products or services in export markets is the selection of the most appropriate range of products to meet the needs of a particular market. Due to rapid technological advances and changes in consumer behaviour, there is a tendency for products to become obsolete and uncompetitive at a faster rate than ever before. In some cases companies who have failed to carry out ongoing research have overlooked the need to keep their product range under constant review, resulting in failure to meet the challenge of both technological changes and the appearance in the market of competitive products from other sources.

The product mix has to be composed of those products which offer the best possible return in relation to the opportunities in the market place. As with all aspects of export marketing, it is important that not too many diverse markets are tackled at any one time. Concentration on a limited range of markets will ease the task of maintaining the best possible range of products for a market, eliminating obsolete lines, possibly modifying products to meet changing market needs and the introduction of new products.

Models and Sizes

It is important to consider the specific needs of each individual market and to be aware of the need to meet specific market requirements regarding both models and sizes on offer.

An obvious example would be the case of motor vehicles which require modification in order to be acceptable in many overseas markets.

The problem of sizes on offer must also be considered. In addition to the need to supply metric sizes in many markets, it should also be remembered that customers' buying habits will frequently necessitate the provision of different sizes, applied to the product itself and especially to the size of the packs on offer.

A major consideration when introducing products into an overseas market will be the need to ensure that any technical or safety regulations are met. Such regulations are subject to frequent changes and invaluable assistance in this area is available from Technical Help for Exporters.

An example of successfully meeting overseas safety standards is provided by Compair Holman, a subsidiary of the Siebe Group which is world famous for its range of portable compressors and exports over sixty per cent of its production. Before the creation of the Single European Market in January 1993, several European markets insisted that only pressure vessels manufactured in their own country could be fitted to portable compressors. This meant that Compair Holman had to buy in these components, which put them at a considerable disadvantage in European markets.

However, with the creation of a Single European Market, the situation was changed by the introduction of a European standard. Compair Holman succeeded in being the first pressure vessel manufacturer in Europe to obtain certification. As a result, the company is now able to fit its own pressure vessels on to portable compressors for sale anywhere in Europe. This enables the company to keep total control over manufacturing processes and quality standards and be more cost effective.

Product Life Cycle

Very frequently the success or failure of an export company will depend on the product policy which is adopted, and this will be governed by the decisions made after analysing the results of market research in order to be in a position to make the right decisions. The basic aim, after completing the market research stage, is to ensure the selection of a product mix composed of those products which optimize the profitability of resources in relation to the opportunities in the market place. An important factor is to appreciate that the length of the product life cycle will vary with each product and each overseas market.

There may be instances where the product life cycle may be extended by entering new export markets. In other words, when a product's life cycle is coming to an end in a given market, it may be possible to extend this profitably by introducing the product into a new market.

The product life cycle covers five distinct phases. The first stage is the introduction. During this stage growth of sales will be gradual due to the lack of awareness of the product in the market place. A high proportion of products fail at this stage and a short life product can be very costly in an overseas market in view of the expense and effort involved in investigating the market and introducing a product for the first time.

If a product survives the introduction stage, the next stage will be the growth stage, when there will be every hope that as the market becomes aware of and accepts the product, growth of sales will accelerate.

It is inevitable that in due course competition will appear in the market and this stage can be described as the maturity stage; it will in time be followed by the fourth stage, saturation.

At this stage, growth in sales will have ceased and increasing competition could lead to a price war and consequent reduction of profitability. The fifth and final stage of the product life cycle is decline, and at this stage a decision must be made on the future of the product. It may be possible to make alterations to the product to extend the life cycle. Alterations could involve such things as improving quality or style, or possibly introducing new features, as has been done in many instances with cameras. With certain products it may be possible to improve performance and possibly reduce costs. This may possibly be achieved by introducing cheaper or alternative materials.

The options available will depend very largely on the product. It may be possible, for example, to meet competition either by a reduction of quality or quantity. Some items may be over-engineered, in which case product modification may enable production costs to be reduced. An alternative to quality modification is quantity reduction. For example in such products as packaged foods or confectionery, it may well be possible to achieve savings in costs by maintaining quality but reducing the quantity per pack.

In the case of some products, it may well be possible to fight growing competition by improving services offered to the customers. Finally, it may be possible to extend a product's life cycle by offering added value through the introduction of pro-motional benefits, such as give-aways, competitions, premiums and holidays.

Alternatively it may be decided to withdraw the product. Should this decision be made there are two options: (1) the product may be eliminated overnight; (2) the price is increased and the demand is allowed to fall away (this option will have the benefit of producing maximum returns during the dying days of the product life cycle).

After taking the decision to eliminate the product, further savings can be made by reducing promotion costs.

In any market it is most important to keep a tight check on a product's life cycle. This is especially true in an overseas market, where an exporter must be ruthless to be successful and eliminate obsolete lines as quickly as possible.

A vital aspect of entering an overseas market is to select the appropriate product mix – the range of products to be offered bearing in mind the need to maintain profitability and optimise distribution and promotion resources.

Because of the high cost of research and development before a product can be introduced in an overseas market, and because of the uncertainty of a product's future, an exporter will frequently set a relatively high price initially. The exporter must obviously find a market segment that will accept this, and

consequently a new product will only be introduced in response to favourable research findings.

When selecting overseas markets, four basic strategies are
available. The first will be to consider the possibility of market
expansion, that is to say to make every effort to increase sales
in existing markets. The second strategy is market development,
which will involve the introduction of existing products into
either new regions of already established markets or breaking
into entirely new markets.

The third possibility is product development, seeking increased sales by developing new products to meet the needs of
existing markets.

Finally the answer may be diversification, which will involve
the development of new products to meet the needs of new
markets.

The introduction of all new products will involve seeking the
answers to the following questions.

Is it a unique product? Such a product is a rarity, but any
   product will be in a strong position if it has one or more
   unique features.
Is the product within 'the business I am in' category?
Can it be manufactured with existing plant, facilities and staff?
   This will obviously be of vital importance.
*Are the present sales force, agents or distributors competent to
   handle sales?*
*Is it a replacement for an existing product, or does it
   complement an existing product?*
*Will it affect sales of an existing product and, if so, to what
   extent?*
What is the projected product life cycle?
Are existing import regulations likely to remain unchanged?
*Can any savings be achieved by improving distribution
   arrangements?*
*Is there any possibility of new technical or safety regulations
   being introduced?*
Is the overseas market's general economy likely to remain stable?

As in the case of the original selection of possible overseas markets, the answers to these questions can be sought by overseas market research involving both desk and field research.

Preliminary planning prior to the introduction of a new product will also necessitate a full review of available resources: executives, managers, salesmen, agents, distributors, production facilities, plant, buildings, customer goodwill and the rest.

In addition to determining all direct costs, an assessment must be made of any necessary investment to cover market research, advertising, publicity, trade fairs, exhibitions or appointment of agents.

When considering a new product launch, it is necessary to go through a series of Go or No go decision points and to draw up a detailed schedule of all the activities leading to a successful launch. It must be emphasized that new products are subject to a high rate of failure, this failure frequently being due to inadequate research or lack of effective cost and time evaluation.

A market profile has to establish initially if a company has previous experience in a market; valuable information will be available from agents, distributors and sales staff. If a new market is involved, a detailed market profile uses market research, market reports and questionnaires.

It will be most important to establish the direct costs involved in the production of a new product and also to investigate the prices of competitors' products. It will be important to assess the additional investment which will be required such as the cost of any new plant and equipment.

Before the launch of a new product it is important to undertake a detailed survey of distribution costs. Insofar as initial delivery to the market is concerned it may be advantageous to make use of the wide range of facilities offered by freight forwarders. Consideration must also be given to establishing the most effective channels of distribution within a market. These will vary considerably for different products and different markets.

It must be remembered that a wide range of import restrictions may exist in different markets. The most usual reason for the imposition of these restrictions is a desire to protect a market's home industries against competition from imported products. Restrictions may also be imposed to save hard currency.

Total Product Concept

When introducing a new product it is frequently beneficial to initiate a test marketing programme. This becomes necessary in view of the high cost of introducing a new product overseas and involves the testing out of a product in a given area which represents as nearly as possible the whole market to be targeted.

Care must be taken in selecting the area for a test marketing operation and this will usually be done in conjunction with an agent or distributor.

The object of the exercise will be to identify any deficiencies or problems, and to establish potential selling points to be developed.

Information gained from a test marketing programme should give a good indication of the likely success to be achieved when the product is finally launched across the whole of the selected market.

Many factors will influence the acceptability of a product in an overseas market. In the case of technical products it is most important to consider, in addition to the basic product, what is known as the total product concept. This means giving detailed attention to a range of ancillary services which may be offered in addition to the core product. For example, it may often attract additional customers if it is possible to offer a range of suitable accessories.

An important feature in obtaining sales for a technical product will be the provision of an installation service. This will usually be undertaken by a local agent or distributor. In the case of major industrial equipment it may be desirable to provide the services of technical experts from the exporting company.

A further factor which will be essential will be the provision of a detailed operating manual. It may be necessary to provide this in the language appropriate to the market in question.

For some industrial equipment, another valuable addition will be the provision of staff and facilities to undertake training of production and maintenance operatives.

Another most important aspect of the total product concept will be the assurance that an adequate supply of spare parts will be made readily available, together with a suitable form of warranty or guarantee. Above all, every effort must be made to ensure the provision of a comprehensive after-sales service.

As will be readily appreciated, when exporting technical products it is absolutely essential to think in terms of the total product concept, considering a wide range of benefits which may be provided for the customer, to enhance the prospects of your product being selected in preference to a competitor's.

Needs of Different Markets

It is most important to appreciate that because you have success with a product in the home market, or even in certain overseas markets, that product will not necessarily be acceptable on a worldwide basis.

Each overseas market must be studied individually. The first point to be established is the possibility of adapting existing products in order to satisfy local needs, tastes and regulations in an overseas market.

A matter of prime importance will be to undertake a detailed study of competition taking into consideration both domestic products and those imported from other sources.

It will be very important to make a survey of possible buyers for your product, considering the items already handled and deciding if these represent competitive products, or possibly your product may be complementary to those already handled, which would obviously be helpful. An example of this would be a manufacturer of fine china, who might well find a successful opening with a retailer handling quality cutlery and glassware.

It is important to make a detailed study of both the economic and the political situation in a market. The dangers of attempting to enter a market with an unstable political or economic situation will be very obvious.

When considering the economic situation, a detailed study

should be made of such matters as tariffs, quality and safety standards, possible import restrictions or currency controls. Any of which could have a dramatic effect on your success or failure in a market.

Different markets have totally different ideas on design and packaging. These factors must be investigated together with consideration of the most appropriate ways of presenting your product.

Consideration must be given to the available means of undertaking advertising and promotion; these problems are discussed fully in chapters 4 and 7.

When establishing a marketing mix, prior to launching a product in a market, it is important to consider both the controllable and the uncontrollable factors.

Detailed below are various factors which fall under these headings.

Controllables:
- Product development
- Price
- Product handling
- Promotion
- Personal selling
- Packing
- Public relations
- Advertising
- Branding
- Channels of distribution
- Display
- Research data, collection and analysis
- Servicing

Uncontrollables:
- Government actions and legislative regulations
- Competitors' activities
- Trade habits and procedures
- Changing consumer habits and customs
- Acts of man, strikes, riots and so on.

It will be essential to be aware of all these factors when planning your approach to a market.

Packing for Export

First and foremost it is important to appreciate the subtle difference in the meaning of the terms packing and packaging.

Packing may be defined as the material needed to protect a product in transit and to ensure that the final package, be it a carton, case or crate, or pallet will be acceptable to the carrier whether for carriage by road, rail, sea or air. Each method of transport will present different packing problems, and increasingly consideration must be given to the possible use of containerization. The growing use of containerization offers many advantages, such as the possibility of using lighter packing, the assurance of protection from pilferage or possible damage by adverse weather conditions.

Whatever may be the most appropriate method of packing for export, this will generate costs and ways of deriving benefits other than mere protection in transit must be considered. It is important to appreciate how packing may be used as a method of identifying and promoting a product. This approach is especially relevant in the case of consumer goods, and it is from this basic idea that the concept of packaging has been derived.

There are many ways in which this objective may be achieved, and some of them will now be considered to illustrate the basic principle. It must however be appreciated that the use of packaging as a marketing tool will depend on many factors such as the product itself and the market to which the product is to be sent. Indeed for some products there may well be a need to vary the packaging for different markets. Furthermore, final choice of suitable packaging will be influenced by the funds available for this aspect of marketing, bearing in mind that some products will be able to support higher costs for promotional packaging, as for example perfumery and toiletries.

When considering promotional material on a package, this may be directed towards the wholesaler, the retailer or the final customer.

The art of packaging and its use as a promotional tool has become a highly specialized operation, and a range of new possibilities has been created by the development of new materials and packaging methods.

Such developments as plastic containers, transparent plastic sheeting, squeeze bottles and aerosols, have helped to bring about a revolution in packaging. A further example of the development of new technologies is various types of bubble pack and shrink wrapping.

Some products with internationally recognizable packaging are, for example, Kodak products, Coca Cola and the '57' symbol established by Heinz.

When determining the most suitable packaging and packing for export, it is important to investigate a range of restrictions which are applied in various markets. An example of such restrictions is the use of on-pack promotional gifts which is not allowed in Venezuela. More recently, Germany has decreed that packing materials must be recyclable. For many years Australia has prohibited the use of straw as a packing material, also un-treated wood. In Saudi Arabia the use of newspapers as a packing material is prohibited, and in Libya green packing material would be regarded as offensive, being the colour of the national flag.

Detailed research must be undertaken to determine any possible problems which may be met in providing acceptable packaging and packing.

The necessary guidance and information is readily available from the Department of Trade and Industry, Trade Associations and Chambers of Commerce.

The factors which must be considered when determining the most appropriate packaging and packing are detailed below.

- Nature of the product.
- Size and weight of the product.
- Total cost of packaging and packing.
- Competition, with special reference to the particular types of packaging used by competitors.
- Customer profile. Certain markets have clearly defined preferences for particular types of packaging, and especially for colours used.
- Restrictions and regulations in the market.
- Political or religious considerations which may prohibit the use of certain colours or symbols.

- For many consumer goods, consideration must be given to the overall configuration and dimensions of a pack, to facilitate display on supermarket shelves.
- Handling and display. For example, for certain products sold in supermarkets, it is sometimes said that 'eyelevel is buy level', referring of course to the suitability of the pack to be displayed at an appropriate level.
- Climatic conditions in overseas market.

In the early days of exporting little thought was given to packing and the usual procedure was merely to protect the products with straw in a crate or case. Today, in order to succeed in the export field, it is imperative that careful consideration be given to all aspects of packing and packaging. Above all, the needs and wishes of the overseas customer must be considered, as well as any restrictions or regulations which may apply in an overseas market.

With reference to acceptability by an overseas customer, an example of changing standards is the packing of china and pottery. For many years the only consideration was the physical protection of the goods in transit. This was usually achieved by packing the goods with straw in wooden crates or casks. Although this provided adequate protection in transit, it frequently provided considerable problems for the customer after receipt of the packages. Unpacking the goods was frequently a lengthy and unpleasant task. After spending time in dockside warehouses and ships' holds, the straw was often damp, smelly and infested with vermin. In such cases not only was the customer faced with an unpleasant task of unpacking the goods, but afterwards had the expensive and time consuming task of cleaning the contents of the packages and also disposing of the packing materials.

From the above example, it is easy to appreciate the benefits of modern methods of packing. For china and pottery, this will usually be in fitted cartons, frequently carrying appropriate promotional material. These may then be shipped in large outer cartons, light cases or pallets. In many instances this type of packing will prove to be ideal for containerization, and will meet the needs of the overseas customer.

As previously mentioned, straw is now unacceptable as a packing material in many countries, even when covered by a disinfection certificate. In instances where fitted cartons may prove to be unsuitable or too expensive for a particular range of products, alternative materials are now available such as shredded paper, wood wool or plastic foam.

When determining the most appropriate form of packing to be used it is important to consider the various ordeals to which packages may be exposed, such as handling on the dockside, loading and unloading, the use of slings or grabs and the possibility of crushing by being stacked under other cargo.

Many of these problems can be minimized by the use of containers. Nevertheless, consideration must be given to the packages' ability to withstand climatic variations, especially extremes of heat, cold, humidity and condensation.

In some markets, packages may be vulnerable to pilferage. Obviously it is important to adopt packing which will deter pilferers. It is wise to avoid giving any information on the outside of packages which could give an indication of the contents. In addition, it may be wise to lessen the danger of shipping marks revealing the consignee's identity to a potential pilferer. If, for example, the customer's name is E.G. Jones & Co. a simple mark such as E.G.J. would be too readily identified by the pilferer, who would be well aware of the type of products normally imported by E.G. Jones & Co.

In such a case, it would be appropriate to make use of totally unrelated initials or possibly a symbol for the shipping mark.

It is, of course necessary for an agreed shipping mark to appear both on the export invoice and on the export packages to enable them to be readily identified during transit, and on arrival at the final destination.

For example a typical shipping mark may be as follows:

A.C.G.
Rosario No.5
Via Buenos Aires

There is a wide range of symbols which are accepted internationally for the marking of packages, details of which are readily available from freight forwarders. In the case of air freight, this may be marked with special labels approved by IATA.

In some markets, customs duties are based on the gross weight of the packages. That is to say, the weight including all internal and external packing materials. Obviously in such markets, the lightest possible form of packing must be used, although the need for adequate protection must take priority.

Colours and symbols may well have very different meanings in different countries, and such points must not be overlooked in order to ensure that your packaging and packing is acceptable in a market. Frequently colours influence product association, and it is well to seek advice on the spot in order to avoid possible problems. This guidance could be obtained either from your customers or from your resident agent where one has been appointed.

For the newcomer to exporting, the services of a specialist contract packer could be invaluable.

Questions for Discussion

1 Explain the stages of a product life cycle.

2 What do you understand by the term 'total product concept'?

3 Describe special factors which must be considered when packing for export.

4

Promotion

Consumer Goods

When planning export promotion, the first essential is to draw up a budget for the various financial outlays which will be incurred.

There are a variety of methods which may be used. A popular one is to allow a percentage of the unit price of a product to be earmarked for promotion. Initially, an estimate must be made of the total sales which it is hoped to achieve in a market and then a calculation of the money to be made available for promotional activities. If it is assumed that a provision of ten per cent will be made available and the sales forecast is for 40,000 units at £3 each, the budget for promotion will be £12,000.

If this method is adopted to fix a promotion budget, it does not necessarily follow that the budget must all be used in a given year. In fact it is prudent to create a promotion budget reserve, placing the agreed percentage of sales into the fund to be used as required. With this method until sales become established, comparatively little money will be available for promotion. This problem may be overcome by spending the agreed budget figure, leaving a deficit to be covered by future sales which materialize as a result of the promotion undertaken. This solution will of course depend upon the making of an accurate initial sales forecast.

An alternative method of fixing a promotion budget is to adopt what is known as the 'task method'. With this method, the exporter will consider and cost an appropriate range of promotional activities designed to obtain the sales target which has been set. Obviously, the proposed budget must be a realistic figure, related to the sales which it is hoped will be achieved.

A third method of arriving at a promotion budget can be referred to as the investment method. In this case, all promotional expenditure is regarded as an investment as if the expenditure would be incurred by the purchase of additional plant and machinery. In other words, projected expenditure on promotion is to be regarded as a capital investment which will hopefully lead to increased future sales.

In considering any of these possible approaches to deciding on an appropriate budget for promotional activities, much will depend on the product, the budgeted sales income and especially the level of competition in the market, together with the long-term market potential.

It must be appreciated that the level of a promotion budget will vary considerably in accordance with the product. In cases like fast moving consumer goods and foodstuffs, the percentage of sales allocated to promotion may well be modest. However, the funds available are likely to be large because these products have a high volume turnover.

At the other end of the scale, the percentage of sales value allocated to promotion will be significantly higher in the case of such products as perfumery and toiletries.

Promotion covers a wide range of activities such as advertising, publicity, films, videos, merchandising displays, trade fairs and sponsorship. The choice of the most suitable vehicles for promotion will of course vary for each type of product, and also in accordance with accepted customs in a particular market.

Industrial Products

The appropriate vehicles for promoting industrial products are different from those used for consumer goods.

In the case of consumer goods promotions, these will be aimed not only at the final consumer, but also at wholesalers and retailers. However, in the case of industrial products, the promotion will be aimed at the individual final user of the product which will frequently be operating in a highly specialized field.

A wide range of opportunities exists for promoting consumer goods and these include press, television and radio, advertising and in-store promotions. For industrial products, the range of possibilities is more limited and will probably be concentrated on specialized trade journals, trade fairs and visits to individual potential users of the product.

For the general promotion of products, the work of the Central Office of Information (COI) should be mentioned. The origin of the Central Office goes back to 1911 when, after the passing of the National Insurance Act, it was established by Lloyd George as a government information service to explain the new legislation to employers.

Exporters have been accustomed to receiving a marvellous service from the COI in support of their export promotions. The role of the Central Office has now changed and its main activity is providing publicity support for the work of the Department of Industry in promoting British trade and with it the interests of exporters.

This role also applies to the production of films and videos which is now carried out entirely for government departments but also provides a service to companies through the Department of Trade and Industry.

It will be readily appreciated that the activities of the Central Office of Information are of special interest to the exporter of industrial products.

Public Relations

The creation of good public relations is a most important factor in launching a successful marketing campaign. This involves the building up of a good relationship not only with the public, the distributors and the customers but above all with the media.

If good relations can be established with the media, invaluable free publicity may be obtained, often covering, for example, such matters as the development of new products or processes, and visits by company executives or specialists to the market. There may well be opportunities to obtain favourable media coverage of such matters as the securing of a new contract, or possibly the provision of guarantees or after-sales service.

Apart from the fact that such coverage is free, favourable comments in the media will often create interest and attention.

Another important aspect of public relations is the establishment of trust and good working arrangements with customers and distributors. If this can be achieved, the company which has established a good working relationship with contacts in a market must be in a favoured position to obtain business. It is not hard to appreciate the advantages which this will afford, compared to a company which has not established any rapport with contacts in the market.

Obviously, matters which may attract favourable comments from the media will vary according to the product and according to the market. However, it is vitally important to be aware of the potential advantages to be obtained from good public relations, and to take full advantage of every opportunity. When considering the issue of a press release, in the hope that it will receive favourable attention from the media, it should be remembered that editors are constantly seeking suitable material and will often show interest in press releases.

In the field of export marketing, public relations in the broadest sense is assuming ever increasing importance.

To achieve success in a market, it is no longer sufficient to design and produce an acceptable product. What is of prime importance is the ability to bring the company and its products to the attention of potential customers. Very often this may be assisted by good on-going public relations.

The effort and expenditure which a company may devote to public relations will, of course, vary in accordance with the product and the company. Nevertheless, the basic fact remains that any company can derive enormous benefits from an appreciation of the value of good public relations. Every aspect of a company's operations may be considered to ensure that the fullest possible publicity be obtained for every aspect of the company and its products.

The major aim will always be to establish a recognized and

respected image for the company, together with the dissemination of technical and any other information to both existing and potential customers.

An example of highly successful public relations are the achievements of Richard Branson primarily in respect of Virgin Atlantic Airways, but also in connection with the company's other activities from popular music to radio stations.

Successful public relations have succeeded in establishing worldwide recognition of the Virgin name.

Sales Literature

Sales literature plays a vital role in establishing a company image. It is wise to appreciate that the first opportunity which a potential customer may have to form an opinion of a company and its products will often be from sales literature. It is important that a company's sales literature be designed specifically to meet the needs and tastes of an individual market.

Obviously, for overseas markets a vital factor will be the presentation of literature in an appropriate language. There is a tendency for some companies to economize by producing multi-lingual literature. There are, of course, instances where this may be acceptable, as for instance in Canada. As a country with two different languages, material in English and French presents no problem. However, in many markets it is important to make the customer feel that an effort has been made to produce literature especially for that market in the appropriate language.

When a decision is taken to produce foreign language material, it is imperative that great attention be given to the translation. A literal translation of the English text will often result in a loss of impact, or even a complete misrepresentation of the facts contained in the original text.

It should be remembered, for example, that the Spanish text for use in Latin America will be quite different from the version which would be acceptable in Spain. Indeed, similar difficulties will arise when considering the use of Portuguese in Portugal or Brazil.

This point can be illustrated by the experience some years ago of the Department of Trade and Commerce in Canada, who produced a handsome publicity booklet in Portuguese to accompany a high level trade mission to Brazil. Fortunately, having produced the draft of the booklet, the department submitted this to their post in Rio de Janeiro seeking their comments. The draft was returned with a total of 123 mistakes carefully circled in red. The majority of the errors reflected the different use of the language in Portugal and Brazil. The booklet would have been fine in Portugal but would have made no sense in Brazil.

Another example of the perils of undertaking translations without expert guidance was also provided by the Canadian Department of Trade and Commerce, who sent to their post in Tokyo an advance draft of a Japanese translation of a booklet which had been prepared in Canada. The Minister (Commercial) in Tokyo displayed great tact and a sense of humour. He sent the Department a sheet from an American magazine which published what purported to be a verbatim reproduction of a Japanese instruction sheet for the guidance of English speaking motorists in Japan. One phrase read 'Tootle the horn melodiously if a pedestrian were in his path'. The Minister gave this example of pidgin English and explained that the text of the proposed booklet would read exactly like that to a Japanese reader.

The examples mentioned emphasize the need to take great care when translating material for use in overseas markets. As a general guide, material should not only be translated by a native speaker, but above all should be submitted to a contact in the overseas market for final approval.

Direct Mail

Despite the fact that recent years have seen a dramatic increase in the use of direct mail as an advertising and promotion tool in the United Kingdom, its use in overseas markets is more limited.

An obvious difficulty is the production of suitable material for distribution to overseas markets. In addition to the basic problem of producing translations which would be meaningful, it is very important to make a close study of the kind of layout, text and artwork which customers in the market are accustomed to in order to devise material which will be acceptable in a given market.

In addition, consideration must be given to two other factors: the question of how to obtain suitable mailing lists as well as the cost of the exercise.

Use of direct mail will be made very much easier if it is possible to organize a direct mail operation with the assistance of an agent or distributor in the market through whom it may be possible to organize the whole exercise.

An example of a situation where a direct mail promotion may be used would be in a case where it is proposed to participate in an overseas trade fair. In such a case, an important first step would be to embark on a direct mail campaign, to inform all possible customers about your plans and your products in the hope that this would be an effective way of stimulating interest and encouraging visitors to your stand.

Merchandising Displays

For the promotion of consumer goods the use of merchandising displays has for some years been growing in popularity.

The concept of in-store promotions originated in the United States and Canada, where for a number of years groups of department stores have mounted promotions of British goods. Having met with considerable success, the scheme has now been adopted in a wide range of markets.

Essentially, arrangements for in-store merchandising displays are made between the exporter and the department store group. Frequently, the store will make a contribution to the cost of the promotion. In many instances the Department of Trade and Industry will extend financial assistance to the store towards the cost of promoting an event. In addition, DTI and commercial staff work closely with the store to ensure that the event receives maximum exposure. This type of promotion is valuable for a wide range of products, such as furniture, china and glassware, clothing and foodstuffs.

For products which do not readily lend themselves to this type of promotion, an alternative possibility is to mount a mobile exhibition. The cost of mounting such a venture is high, but the potential value of a mobile exhibition, which can be mounted over a period of time in a number of venues is considerable for certain types of products. Such a venture would be suitable, for example, to display a range of specialized technical products and equipment to selected buyers.

Participation in an overseas promotion exercise is expensive, and the choice of the most appropriate type of promotion will depend on both the product and the chosen market. This is an instance where valuable guidance may be obtained from the Department of Trade and Industry, also from various trade associations and chambers of commerce.

Trade Fairs

Trade fairs present an excellent opportunity to promote products in overseas markets.

The Department of Trade and Industry provides both practical and financial support when an exporter exhibits at an overseas trade fair as part of the United Kingdom group.

The main services offered are the following.

1 organized group support at selected exhibitions overseas;
2 group participation through trade associations and chambers of commerce;
3 reduced participation rates for space and stand construction;
4 support from departmental exhibition experts and group sponsors.

If the event is outside Western Europe, exhibitors in the group may be eligible for travel grants.

Assistance at overseas trade fairs is provided through the joint venture scheme, where an approved sponsor, normally a trade association or chamber of commerce will recruit a group of United Kingdom exporters to exhibit at an agreed overseas trade fair.

Valuable information is available from the Department of Trade and Industry's overseas trade magazine which provides regular news of export practice, opportunities and support services. It is mailed to United Kingdom exporters free of charge, ten times a year. A supplement, the Promotions Guide, gives details of forthcoming supported events including overseas trade fairs, store promotions, inward and outward missions.

Trade fairs are promoted to cover a very wide range of products and services, and it is obviously important to select those trade fairs which are most suitable for your own special needs. It should be remembered that guidance and assistance is available to make the right selection, not only from the Department of Trade, but especially from trade associations, chambers of commerce and export clubs who have had previous experience of these fairs and frequently act as sponsors to form acceptable groups which will qualify for DTI assistance.

There are many products for which participation in an overseas trade fair provides a unique opportunity to get first hand experience of a market and to make personal contact with potential customers. This is of special importance, for example, in the case of capital goods.

Before taking part in an overseas trade fair, it is very important to undertake market research in order to gain a clear indication of the possibilities which may exist in a market, together with a detailed understanding of the market and its special needs. The preliminary research is vital in order to have the best possible opportunity of getting favourable results from participation in an overseas trade fair. One of the worst mistakes which an exporter can make is to assume that merely exhibiting a range of samples in an overseas market automatically ensures success.

Before even deciding to participate, it is necessary to investigate every aspect of the market covering such factors as product acceptability, price ranges prevailing in the market and generally accepted channels of distribution. In addition, it is important to investigate any possible restrictions in the market which may affect your product.

When investigating channels of distribution, consider possible initial entry into the market as well as the prospects for establishing a permanent market presence. For example, can this be achieved with the appointment of a number of distributors, or will the best results be obtained by the appointment of a resident agent?

In many cases the appointment of a resident agent will prove to be invaluable to obtain the maximum benefit from participation in the trade fair.

A vital contribution which a resident agent will be able to make will be in assisting with the organization of your stand at a trade fair abroad. It will be important for someone from head office to monitor both the presentation and the follow up. However, in these areas the services of a resident agent will be invaluable.

It frequently happens that because a manufacturer has established a reputation or a brand image in certain markets, the assumption is made that mere participation in an overseas trade fair will automatically ensure success. However, being unknown in the market the exporter will need to publicize its participation and initiate appropriate advertising and public relations back up prior to the exhibition.

To obtain the maximum benefit from participation, it is very important, after undertaking initial market research, to draw up a clearly defined marketing plan.

Having taken a decision to exhibit overseas, it is important to consider not only the products to be exhibited, but above all to ensure that qualified staff will be available to staff the stand. The staff will require comprehensive product knowledge, and they must also be fully briefed on the company's marketing policy and have complete fluency in the appropriate language. Due consideration must also be given to local customs, as a lack of knowledge of cultural differences can cause offence.

Assuming that an exporter completes successful initial research and exhibits acceptable products, supported by capable staff on the stand, there remains a vital aspect which may so easily be overlooked: the importance of appreciating that the marketing effort does not stop with the closing of the exhibition. Participation in an overseas trade fair should be looked upon as a first class opportunity to carry out overseas research and to establish contacts in a market, and it is vital that no effort be spared to ensure that a detailed follow up operation is undertaken in order to obtain maximum benefit from the venture.

In a case where business has been obtained at an overseas trade fair, it is important that all orders be given priority to ensure that delivery promises are kept, as broken delivery promises will very quickly destroy any goodwill which may have been created.

It is to be hoped that participation will generate a number of enquiries and it is most important that all such enquiries are fully recorded and followed up immediately after the fair ends.

Promotional Films

In recent years, promotional films and videos have assumed growing importance as a marketing tool. For a wide range of products the contribution to the marketing effort which is made by samples and appropriate literature has been greatly assisted by the use of films and videos.

Some years ago, film as a promotional medium was mainly used for heavy industrial products where size and complexity prevented physical displays at specialist trade fairs and presentations of the actual product to potential overseas customers. In such instances the use of promotional films provided a useful additional marketing tool, not only to display the products, but also to generate an awareness of and interest in the production facilities of the exporter.

However, the possibilities for using this promotional tool for an ever-growing range of products have been greatly increased with the availability of camcorders. Videos provide an excellent opportunity to assist the efforts of overseas agents and representatives to present both specific products and to help with the presentation of a company image to potential customers overseas.

Reference has already been made to the invaluable role played by the Central Office of Information in the distribution and showing of films and videos to selected audiences overseas.

In a number of overseas markets, the cinema still provides a good outlet for certain promotional films. It will be appreciated that the use of cinema promotions will be particularly valuable in markets where television and national newspapers are not widely available.

Visits to Customers

An essential element of an overseas marketing campaign is the need to establish and develop personal contacts with overseas customers.

Even if an exporter has appointed an overseas agent, a number of distributors or even a subsidiary company overseas, their efforts will be greatly strengthened by appropriate members of the marketing staff making frequent visits to a market in order to establish and maintain that all-important personal contact.

Such visits enable the company to keep every aspect of the local situation under review and serve to strengthen bonds which have been made with overseas customers. Properly planned visits to an overseas market will be much appreciated by overseas customers and will provide an invaluable opportunity to obtain personal impressions of the situation in a market, against which to weigh performance. In addition to the favourable impression which this will create with customers, underlining the exporter's determination to research and meet the needs of a market, it will also strengthen links with an overseas agent and encourage its future efforts.

Above all, such visits are invaluable to strengthen customers' confidence and generate goodwill by confirming the exporter's interest in and concern for a market. The cost of such visits is high but there can be no substitute for personal visits and the establishment of face to face contact with overseas customers.

In some markets, an easy mistake is to confine visits to capital cities and major centres. However, for certain products it is well worth considering making more extended market visits spread across the country to customers who may rarely be visited by their overseas suppliers. Such visits will normally be very well received and will usually be profitable.

For a wide range of products, a market where such extended visits could prove profitable would be, for example, Brazil. Due to the huge size of the country, a visit to Rio de Janeiro and Sao Paulo, although both major commercial centres, would mean ignoring the vast potential in other areas of the country.

Whatever option an exporting company adopts, the basic fact of life is that to be successful, an export marketing executive must make frequent visits to overseas customers.

Sponsorship

Reference has already been made to the benefits which can be obtained from good public relations, which can provide a valuable source of free promotion. In chapter seven, the question of normal paid advertising is dealt with in detail.

However, mention must now be made of sponsorship which is not in itself specific advertising of a product or device but can prove to be a most valuable promotional tool.

A growing number of activities are currently sponsored by a wide range of manufacturers, the most common activities to receive sponsorship being sports. An example being the Barclays Bank sponsorship of the football league. In addition, many individual athletes receive sponsorship.

More recently, sponsorship has spread to television programmes, examples being Rumpole of the Bailey sponsored by Croft Port, and certain ITV weather forecasts, sponsored by Legal and General Insurance.

Obviously, sponsorship of major events, such as those mentioned above, or, for example, motor racing, which is heavily sponsored, is a very expensive undertaking and raises the question of why companies should wish to become involved in sponsorship.

The object of the exercise is to promote a public awareness of a company or a brand name. Although sponsorship cannot be claimed to be the same as specific advertising campaigns to promote a product or service, it undoubtedly succeeds in keeping a company or brand name in the public eye. An example of an industry where enormous resources have been devoted to sponsorship is the manufacture of cigarettes. With the imposition of various restrictions on cigarette advertising, many brand names are now linked with a wide variety of sponsorships which undoubtedly ensure that the brand names are continually brought to the attention of the public.

Although it is easy to think of sponsorship as being a useful promotional tool, but one which involves heavy expenditure, restricting its use to major companies, often with internationally known names, there are opportunities for smaller companies to undertake sponsorship on a more modest scale. In either case, the justification remains the same, to keep the name of a product or company in the public eye.

Questions for Discussion

1 Describe the steps which you would take to promote industrial products.

2 Explain what you understand by public relations.

3 What special factors must be considered when preparing sales literature for use overseas.

5

Pricing

Direct Production Costs

When establishing a selling price it is necessary to take a wide range of factors into consideration.

The first consideration is the basic cost of manufacturing a product. Obviously, due consideration must be given to the cost of raw materials, also the direct labour costs involved. A further important factor to consider is the allocation of overheads. Methods vary for apportioning overheads to a particular product, but it is important to devise a scheme whereby an appropriate percentage of a company's total overhead costs may be apportioned to each item produced.

It is necessary to have a clear understanding of all the costs which will be incurred for any given product. In addition to covering the cost of labour and materials, it is essential to make provision for indirect costs and overheads such as, for example, plant and building maintenance, rent, rates, heating, lighting, insurance, bank interest, stationery, telephones, packing, vehicles, advertising and promotion, depreciation and professional charges. Indirect material costs and expenses must cover such items as consumable stores, lubricants, cleaning materials and small tools.

Consideration must also be given to covering internal administration expenses, such as managerial, executive and general office expenses, direct office costs and postage.

In arriving at a price, provision must be made to ensure that all selling expenses are covered, such as sales office staff, cost of travellers, commissions and travelling expenses, publicity expenses, discounts, preparation of samples, drawings and designs and preparation of quotations.

At one time, some manufacturers tended to dispose of surplus production in overseas markets, frequently at unrealistic prices. Although this approach is no longer possible, it is important to appreciate the problems presented by competitors. There have been instances of would be exporters taking a home market price and merely adding on freight and insurance. This amateurish approach could very easily result in prices being unrealistically high, or in some cases too low by ignoring the situation in the market and not appreciating what price the market will bear.

Buyers in overseas markets will be considering quotations from a number of sources and selecting the most competitive quotation. It is therefore vital to consider costs very carefully when fixing an export price, ensuring that you quote the most competitive figure, commensurate with a reasonable profit, in the hope of achieving maximum sales in an overseas market. It should be borne in mind that it is important to offer quality products at competitive prices.

When deciding on a selling price it is also important to deal specifically with the product for export, appreciating that some of the costs which apply to products for the home market will not necessarily apply to exports.

Although export prices must be competitive, it has to be remembered that particularly low prices must not contravene any anti-dumping laws which may be in operation in the overseas market.

Promotion Costs

There are different ways in which provision can be made to cover the costs of promotion.

Obviously, to make an impact in an overseas market, a measure of promotion will be essential. In many instances, the normal practice will be to include the cost of overseas promotion in the total cost of distribution. However, in some cases, provision will be made to cover special selling aids for a product leaving the other promotion costs to be included in the company's general provision for advertising and publicity.

The problem will vary in accordance with the product and the market. However when calculating prices for export, it is essential to include adequate provision to cover the additional costs which will be incurred to promote a product abroad.

An essential aspect of overseas promotion is advertising. Here again, many methods are available and these are explained in detail in chapter 7. It must however, be emphasized that full allowance must be made for the cost of advertising when building up an export selling price.

Distribution Costs

The cost of distribution is a major factor in arriving at a selling price, and the method of determining distribution costs will vary according to the products concerned.

Initially, the cost of transport to the chosen port of shipment must be calculated. A product which would create the least problems would be a standard mass produced product which would be the same for every market, as for example washing powders. In such an example, it would usually be possible to establish a standard percentage uplift on the production cost to cover transport to the port of shipment. It may be found that an addition of ten per cent to the production cost will cover the cost of internal transport to the port of loading, either by the exporter's own transport, outside hauliers or rail as appropriate, also covering insurance and any related documentation up to the FOB (Free on Board) stage. In such an example, the ten per cent uplift would be applied irrespective of the port used. The differences between this allowance and the actual cost of a specific delivery could be so insignificant as not to warrant individual costing.

However, the above method would be quite inappropriate for many items which account for a major proportion of exports such as heavy engineering products, possibly requiring special handling and transport arrangements. For this type of product, each shipment will have to be considered separately in order to ensure that all delivery costs are covered in the selling price.

Much of the cost of dispatching goods to a port increases with bulk and weight. However, from the receipt of an order to the final shipment of the goods, the paper work varies very little. The necessary form filling for an order worth £6,000 will be much the same as for an order worth only £60.

The costs previously referred to apply when quoting an FOB price (in other words, the cost of the goods delivered 'Free on Board'). However, further items of cost must be considered when the quotation is cost, insurance and freight (CIF). The major additional items of costs will be freight, insurance and any further incidental costs which may be incurred.

A vitally important factor to remember is that, however the price is quoted by the exporter to the overseas customer, every effort must be made to keep these costs as low as possible as they must all be passed on to the final customer and will affect the product's competitiveness.

A major factor to be investigated will be the cost of distributing products in an overseas market. Methods and costs will vary but it is important to make a thorough investigation of the options available in each market. For example, will your products be sold direct to the consumer? Will distribution be through selected retail outlets? Will products be distributed through wholesalers?

As will be appreciated, whichever option is chosen, it will have a significant effect on the price of the product to the final customer.

The aim of effective distribution is to ensure that products reach the final outlet in good condition at the right time and at the right price. This makes it very important to pay particular attention to every aspect of the cost of distribution. This must be kept under constant review to ensure use of the most efficient method of distribution. When considering the total costs incurred to sell your products overseas, arrangements must be made to take into account any handling or storage charges which may be incurred.

In addition, consideration must be given to any duties or tariffs which may be imposed and these must also be taken into account when considering the final cost of your product to an overseas customer.

Competitors' Prices

An important factor to be considered when determining export selling prices is the price being offered by your competitors. Obviously, this may not be easy to discover, but the problems may be eased in markets where you have a resident agent. The appointment of overseas agents is covered in detail in chapter 6, but at this stage it can be established that one of the most important responsibilities of an overseas agent is to provide the exporter with a constant flow of market intelligence, providing detailed information on the activities of your competitors, especially details of their products and prices.

In chapter 4, reference was made to participation in overseas trade fairs, and it must be stressed that such participation will provide an excellent opportunity to gain valuable information on prices being offered by your competitors. When considering competition in a market, it is helpful to consider competitors' catalogues and promotional material, which will be readily available at a trade fair.

When meeting price competition there are a number of options which are available. Obviously it may be possible to reduce the FOB price, or consider if economies can be made, for example by reducing freight costs by making larger shipments thereby reducing freight costs per unit. The problem will vary according to the products and the market, but it will be important to make a detailed costing of the physical distribution of your products in an overseas market.

It must be remembered that every aspect of transporting your products to an overseas market and distribution within that market will influence the final price of your goods. Hence any unjustified distribution costs may result in losing a market to more efficient competitors.

In order to minimize distribution costs, it is important to keep abreast of changes and developments. This will be particularly important in the area of through transport to overseas markets, making savings by the use of unit loads, cargo groupage, and containerization. In this area, invaluable assistance is available from freight forwarders.

A valuable source of information is the Department of Trade and Industry through their Market Information Enquiry Service. Use of this service can help to establish the prospects for specific products in a chosen market, suggesting not only how to sell into the market, but also who should be approached.

Cost of Packing

In chapter 3, various packing options were considered. Whatever method is chosen as the most appropriate for a particular product, consideration must be given to the effect which the cost of packing and the choice of packing methods will have both on freight charges and on the final selling price. Furthermore, it is important to take into consideration the various restrictions which may be imposed in some markets.

Obviously, the basic essentials are to ensure the safe arrival of products overseas and, where possible, to consider the possible use of packaging as a promotional tool. For all products, it is necessary to provide suitable protection for the journey. However, additional costs will be incurred if it is necessary to take extra precautions against such factors as intense heat or cold, humidity or condensation.

For a newcomer to exporting, it may well be wise to obtain quotations from specialist contractors who have the necessary expertise and specialize in packing for export.

There will be considerable differences in the cost of packing when considering shipments by sea or by air freight. In view of the cost of additional packing for sea freight, it may be possible to consider air freight for some products. In such an event it will be possible to use much lighter packing as the products will be subject to less handling. In addition, savings may be made, especially in the case of smaller consignments, by using the services of a freight forwarder to consolidate your goods with other shipments to the same destination, thereby effecting savings in freight charges. This is, of course, in addition to the savings which may be made by using less substantial packing for air freight.

One example of a means of reducing freight charges is provided by Coca Cola. Although the product is available worldwide, the cost of packing and transporting bottles or cans would almost certainly render the overseas selling price totally uncompetitive. The problem has been solved by exporting only the essence, to be processed by approved bottlers overseas.

Or again, when exporting galvanized tanks, the manufacturers found that freight charges, based on measurements, were extremely high. This problem was overcome by undertaking a cooperative venture with other manufacturers, who were able to use the galvanized tanks as a first class medium for packing and protecting their own products. For example, manufacturers of items as varied as biscuits and pottery use tanks in which to pack and export their products, having the additional benefit of enabling the tank manufacturers to avoid paying heavy freight charges on a large empty tank, based on measurements.

State of Demand

The state of demand in a market will have a significant effect on the selling price of a product. In a case where a new product is introduced, it may be decided to capitalize on the demand for something which is new and does not face any immediate competition. In such a case it may be decided to undertake a period of price skimming, that is to say, to introduce the product at an artificially high price and thereby obtain maximum benefit from the introduction of the new product, for which research has indicated that there is a demand. After the initial demand has been satisfied, and possibly competitive products have appeared, this competition will be met by making a price reduction.

Alternatively, there may well be instances when it is decided to enter a market and compete with a number of existing products. In such a case, a policy of penetration pricing may be adopted, introducing the product at the lowest possible price in the hope of establishing a foothold in the market with the introduction of a new product.

Profit Margins

Mention has been made of the factors which must be taken into account when arriving at a possible selling price for a product in an overseas market.

Having considered the various cost factors, and taken into account all indirect costs, the next factor to consider is what profit margin a product will bear. In the case of many fast-moving consumer goods the profit margin per item may be modest, but this will be compensated for by a high volume of turnover.

Inevitably the profit margin which a product will bear will depend largely on the product. However, there will be instances where products will be able to bear a high profit margin. This will frequently be the case with products which are able to command a premium price. For example, in some markets a high level of profit may be obtained if the product is one which is regarded as a luxury item, for which people expect to pay a high price. In some instances, prices may be artificially high if there is a large demand for a product which is in short supply.

In a market such as the United States, there is frequently a willingness to pay a higher price for an imported product, which may be considered superior to domestic products. Examples would be such items as high quality clothing, unusual quality food products, whisky and certain items of china and glassware.

Credit Risks

In chapter 6 a number of methods of selling goods abroad are described. However, whatever option is taken consideration must be given to the credit risks involved, and steps must be taken to minimize and if possible eliminate these risks.

The vital fact to remember is that the most important aspect of overseas trade is to take the necessary steps to ensure that payment will be received, preferably without undue delay.

It will be appreciated that it may well be more difficult to establish the credit worthiness of a customer overseas than would be the case in the home market. It is therefore advisable to take advantage of the facilities described below, in order to minimize credit risks.

The Department of Trade and Industry operates an Overseas Status Report Service (OSRS) to help in determining if an overseas company can provide a secure business opportunity. In using this service, a report on the overseas company is prepared by diplomatic service staff, providing up-to-date information from staff who have the necessary local knowledge. In addition, the service provides details of the overseas company's business activities, in order to assist the exporter in deciding whether to pursue business possibilities with a potential customer overseas.

In preparing these reports, the commercial department of the diplomatic service post will normally visit the overseas organization and then be in a position to report on the company's trading interests and capabilities, the scope of its activities, what territory it can cover, together with details of its warehousing and distribution facilities. Further information will be provided about its sales force, also technical knowhow and facilities for providing after-sales service. The report will give an indication of financial status and resources, although this will not be a formal credit rating.

Payment from overseas customers involves different procedures from those used in the home market, and it is most important that an exporter be fully aware of the procedures involved. It is inevitable that credit risks exist in every market, also the exporter faces additional risks such as the possible imposition of credit controls, also political risks which can prevent payments being made. It is very important to consider taking credit insurance cover against these risks. The Export Credits Guarantee Department (ECGD) can help to insure against the risks of not being paid for your exports. In addition, the department provides guarantees to banks for exporters of capital goods, under which finance may be obtained for export business, usually at a favourable rate of interest.

In chapter 6, a variety of ways are described in which overseas trade may be conducted. A further option to consider is factoring. Here, for a fee, the factoring company undertakes the task of securing payment from the overseas customer, and usually guarantees up to eighty per cent of the debt to be paid at an early date after shipment of the goods. Use of this facility will, of course, reduce the profit margin but it may still be considered a valuable option for certain markets. For many years, factoring has played a significant role in trade in the United States.

Factoring is a financial operation, which has grown considerably in recent years; it is applied not only to home market transactions but especially to the export trade. An additional benefit which the service offers to the exporter is that by employing a factor, the exporter reduces its export sales ledger to a single account. The exporter is thereby relieved of the need to provide specialist staff to handle accounts for overseas customers. The factoring company will provide the exporter with a specific quotation for its services, based on the amount of work and risk involved.

Agents' Commission

In chapter 6, detailed information is given on the selection and appointment of agents, also the procedures for drawing up an agency agreement.

However, at this stage it is necessary to be aware of the additional costs which will be incurred by making use of an overseas agent. An agent will usually be paid an agreed rate of commission, which may be on a fixed or sliding scale.

The term, for export trade, usually refers to a commission agent. There are, however, other types of agents who may be appointed. For example, a Del Credere agent will be responsible for his customers' bad debts, a responsibility which is not assumed by a commission agent. Understandably, a Del Credere agent will be paid a higher rate of commission than the more usual commission agent.

Whichever type of agent is appointed, due provision must be made to cover not only the cost of commission to be paid, but also any other agent's expenses which an exporter may agree to meet, such as advertising and promotion which may be organized by an agent.

Questions for Discussion

1 List any six items which must be taken into consideration, in addition to the cost of labour and materials, when costing a product.

2 State how you would establish promotion costs for a product.

3 What steps would you recommend to minimize credit risks involved in overseas trade.

6

Selling

Sales Forecasts

An important aspect of a marketing campaign is the preparation of a sales forecast which will be a key factor in any marketing plan. A most important aspect of a sales forecast is that it must be accurate, and above all attainable, in the light of all the facts which will be considered when drawing up the forecast. A common fault with some sales forecasts is a tendency to be over-optimistic, and this will inevitably lead to future problems which may be very difficult to correct. A sales forecast must be based on hard facts, and realistic projections.

The first factor which must be considered is past sales performance. Obviously if the new sales forecast is for use in a market where the company is already operating, a wealth of information will be available from in-company records. In the case of a new market, it may well be possible to make realistic projections based on previous experience in similar markets and on a realistic appraisal of the information which has been obtained from specific research in the chosen market.

Any plans for the introduction of new products should be taken into consideration when drawing up a sales forecast. These will affect the forecast and it is important not to be over-optimistic about the possible sales of a new product. By starting with a modest forecast, any sales which may be forthcoming over and above the original forecast will be a bonus.

Consideration must be given to the planned level of promotional support. This will obviously have an important impact on the sales forecast, especially in the case of new products or new markets.

The economic and political outlook in a market must be considered after undertaking the necessary market research. It would be foolhardy to produce a promising sales forecast where there were doubts about either the economic or political stability of a market.

Reference has previously been made to profit margins, and the profit contribution which may be expected must be borne in mind when drawing up a sales forecast.

Inevitably, a further factor which must be explored fully is the available production capacity. It will be readily appreciated that it would be totally unrealistic to make a sales forecast without first ensuring the availability of adequate production capabilities.

In addition to studying the importance of the economic outlook, attention must be given to prevailing sales trends, based on company records and all available external sources such as the Department of Trade and Industry and banks.

Finally, consideration must be given to marketing costs. With any sales forecast, the marketing costs involved in achieving sales must be considered.

Selling Expenses

Consideration has already been given to the basic components which must be considered when arriving at an export selling price.

There are other expenses which may well be incurred in the promotion of a product overseas such as organizing a special promotion or press conference to launch a product. In chapter 7 the question of advertising is covered in detail and, as will be appreciated, this will frequently prove to be a major source of expense.

Quoting in a Foreign Currency

In times of growing competition it may be necessary to consider the possibility of quoting in a foreign currency. Such a step may well be attractive to the customer overseas but, before considering this method of quoting, attention must be given to both the possible advantages and disadvantages.

The first point to be considered is the stability of the foreign currency. In some markets which have a stable currency and exchange rates, it may well be an advantage to quote overseas customers in their own currency. This will be a considerable incentive to overseas buyers to place their business with you, as they will be relieved of any problems of currency conversions or possible exchange rate variations.

From the exporter's point of view the most obvious risk of quoting in a foreign currency is the possibility of adverse exchange rate fluctuations. In view of this, the number of markets where quoting in a foreign currency will be a worthwhile option will be limited.

Export Quotation Terms

Many options are available to the exporter who must select the appropriate method, bearing in mind that above all it must be acceptable to the overseas customer, especially in the light of the methods adopted by competitors.

In order to avoid any misunderstanding, the International Chamber of Commerce has drawn up a set of the most commonly used 'Terms of Delivery' in international trade. These are known as Incoterms 1990 and cover the thirteen most commonly used terms. Each term places specific and clearly defined responsibilities on both seller and buyer, and is recognized across the world.

Detailed below are the thirteen internationally accepted 'Terms of Delivery' in international trade.

EXW   Ex works
FCA   Free carrier

FAS	Free alongside ship
FOB	Free on board
CFR	Cost and freight
CIF	Cost, insurance and freight
CPT	Carriage paid to –
CIP	Carriage and insurance paid to –
DAF	Delivered at frontier
DES	Delivered ex ship
DEQ	Delivered ex quay
DDU	Delivered duty unpaid
DDP	Delivered duty paid

Types of Sales Organization

Detailed below are some of the most common types of sales organization which may be used for overseas trade.

1 Home-based travelling representative selling direct to retail outlets or industrial users in markets abroad.
2 Home-based travelling representative working with foreign sales agents or local distributors, assisting and supervising their efforts.
3 United Kingdom nationals resident abroad, supervising sales agents and distributors.
4 United Kingdom nationals resident abroad, supervising sales branches, tendering for foreign contracts or selling to overseas governments.
5 Foreign nationals directly employed by the exporter and operating in any of the above mentioned methods.

In addition to the above mentioned methods of organizing overseas trade, attention should be paid to the wide range of alternative options which are described below.

Export merchants purchase goods from suppliers and then sell these products to overseas customers. This provides an opportunity for a newcomer to exporting to sell goods abroad without encountering any of the usual problems associated with export trade. The major advantage for the manufacturer, apart from the opportunity of selling his goods abroad, is that the transaction becomes a normal home market transaction. All responsibility for eventual overseas sales rests with the export merchant. From the manufacturer's point of view the major disadvantage is that he has no contact whatsoever with the customer overseas.

In some cases merchants will specialize. This may be specialization in products as, for example, woollens, cotton piece goods, plastics, textile or engineering products. Similarly merchants may elect to specialize in markets such as Latin America, Africa, the Far East or the United States.

In some instances an export merchant will receive enquiries from overseas customers and will then offer goods to meet the client's specifications. Alternatively, the merchant may receive indents from his overseas customer and then organize purchases from a suitable supplier.

The merchant purchases goods from a supplier as a normal home market transaction, and then sells the goods overseas, arranging shipping and insurances. A merchant company will have an excellent knowledge of the requirements of its customers overseas.

Dealing through export merchants has both advantages and disadvantages. Such trade may well be useful for a manufacturer wishing to find buyers for either surplus production or possibly for frustrated exports due to cancellation of licences or other causes.

With his wide knowledge of overseas markets, the merchant may have a much better opportunity of locating overseas buyers. There may even be instances where some potential markets may not be directly open to the manufacturer, but could be open to a merchant. For example, a merchant importing goods from Eastern Europe may be able to place United Kingdom exports on a barter basis.

There are however disadvantages to be considered. Apart from the lack of direct contact with the overseas customer, the exporter will have no control over the ultimate selling price of his goods, which may well jeopardize the prospect of obtaining repeat orders.

Confirming houses are responsible for a significant amount of export trade. In the case of a confirming house, an overseas customer will place an order to be confirmed by and paid for by the confirming house.

In effect, the confirming house is acting as an agent for the overseas buyer, to look after his orders to manufacturers or suppliers in the United Kingdom. A number of other names may be used to describe a confirming house, such as export house, buying house, shipper or indent house.

Normally the manufacturer will quote Free on Board prices to the confirming house who will then assume responsibility for arranging shipment. The confirming house will take the manufacturer's FOB invoice and then add freight and insurance plus commission and any special disbursements. Any special documentation will be prepared by the confirming house in collaboration with the manufacturer.

The accounts between the manufacturer and the confirming house will usually be operated on a monthly basis, in the same way as a normal home market account. In due course the confirming house will be paid by the overseas customer.

The rate of commission charged by a confirming house to an overseas buyer may vary between two and a half and seven and a half per cent.

Unlike the export merchant, the use of a confirming house does not deprive the exporter of direct contact with the overseas customer. It is, in fact, a method of trade in which the overseas customer, the confirming house and the exporter all work together.

The question may be raised 'Why should an overseas buyer choose to work through a confirming house?' Quite simply, by placing orders for confirmation and payment by a confirming house, it simplifies matters for the overseas customer who may be making purchases from a wide range of different suppliers.

For the exporting manufacturer there can be significant advantages in dealing with customers who use an intermediary in the United Kingdom. Much of the expertise required in the administration of exporting will be provided by the intermediary and detailed queries can be dealt with quickly and conveniently. Detailed overleaf are some of the advantages to be gained by dealing through an intermediary in the United Kingdom.

Factor	Dealing with United Kingdom intermediary	Dealing direct
Quotations	At most, Free on Board.	Importers expect Cost, Insurance and Freight quotation,which involves special knowledge of airfreight, marine and possibly war risk insurance.
Packing	Any special requirements will be specified by intermediary.	Often left to exporter to decide.
Payment	In United Kingdom, paid in sterling.	Problems of dealing with foreign exchange, need to meet exchange control regulations.
Finance	Usually monthly account.	Exporter expected to extend credit terms.
Documentation	Manufacturer only supplies basic details for intermediary to prepare export documentation.	Manufacturer would require trained staff with specialized knowledge.
Risks	Any problems resolved through United Kingdom courts.	Possible problems of action in foreign courts, under foreign laws.
Rapid contact	Manufacturer can offer by telephone and get a prompt reply.	Offer and acceptance can take longer to become effective.
Buffering	Intermediary may carry stocks to meet seasonal demand fluctuation.	Manufacturer may have difficulty in meeting sudden unexpected demand.
Marketing	Market research and promotion undertaken by intermediary.	All these activities fall to exporter.

The following factors must be considered when selling direct to the overseas customer. First and foremost the exporter must set up his own specialized export staff, to be able to prepare Cost, Insurance and Freight invoices and organize insurance against credit risks. It will also be necessary to set up a specialist packing department.

Even after making provision to cover the above costs, the exporter who deals direct with overseas customers will either be able to increase his profit or possibly increase turnover by passing on to the overseas buyer the savings made by eliminating an intermediary.

Usually the major advantage of dealing direct is that the exporter is immediately in closer touch with the overseas market, and will have first hand knowledge of and contact with the market.

Having direct contact with the overseas customer provides an opportunity for establishing a name overseas and is invaluable when any after sales service is required. Direct contact with the overseas customer will facilitate the resolution of any problems which may arise, especially in the case of technical problems.

In some cases a manufacturer may decide to appoint a concessionaire in a market. A concessionaire is usually expert in a particular field and will be granted special authority by a manufacturer to work in a particular market area, usually on a basis of exclusivity. In many cases such an arrangement will produce regular business. However, having no direct contact with the final buyer, channels of distribution will be restricted to the activities of the concessionaire.

There are instances when two or more manufacturers of compatible products will work together to achieve a common purpose, by undertaking a group sales arrangement. Benefits may be obtained by sharing marketing and promotion costs.

A development of the group sales concept is the creation of consortia. This usually happens when there is an opportunity to bid for large tenders overseas, governing such projects as the construction of dams, railways, bridges or power stations. These large-scale projects call for cooperation between many exporters. Frequently, the initiative to set up a consortium will come from firms of consulting engineers. Large-scale projects of this type can frequently be financed with the aid of Export Credits Guarantee Department backed guarantees.

Many of the large department stores in the United States and Canada buy so much from the United Kingdom that they find it pays to set up their own buying offices in this country.

The advantages to a United Kingdom exporter of dealing with a local buying office are that it can secure prompt acceptance of his offers, and is saved the time and expense which would otherwise be involved in visiting the markets.

An export of growing importance is the export of knowhow. In many markets which lack the technical knowledge or expertise to manufacture certain products, there is a growing market for knowhow which would cover for example the sale of manufacturing techniques, blueprints, processes covered by patents, in addition to the installation of plant, quality control systems and the training of operatives.

From the exporter's point of view, this may provide a means of entry to a market where direct exporting would not be possible. In addition there may be an opportunity to extend the life cycle of a product.

One method of exporting knowhow is by entering into a licensing agreement with a manufacturer overseas. The licensor will receive a suitable sum for the licence to produce certain products, either by way of royalties or a percentage of annual turnover or a combination of both. Licences may be granted to overseas manufacturers to use certain trade processes or produce patented products. From the licensor's point of view he must monitor the situation to ensure that the licensee exploits the market fully and also maintains an approved level of quality.

An example of this type of operation was the granting of a licence by the Wilkinson Sword company to a manufacturer in Poland to produce Wilkinson Sword razor blades in Poland. An additional provision in this instance was an agreement by Wilkinson Sword to import an agreed quantity of the finished product.

Another method of exporting knowhow is by entering into a franchising agreement with a company overseas. Franchising would normally be used for a product which cannot itself be patented.

An example of a successful franchising operation is Kentucky Fried Chicken. In this case the franchisor provides the production knowhow, ingredients and other instructions, in addition to staff training and assistance with the provision of appropriate premises and publicity. The franchisee will pay a fee for the franchise and must maintain standards set by the franchisor. A further example of successful franchising is the Body Shop.

In some cases knowhow may be the sale of management services. An example of this is Hilton Hotels, where the hotel pays a fee for the use of the name and above all the acquisition of appropriate management expertise and guidance.

As will be appreciated from the foregoing examples, the export of knowhow does not only apply to developing countries. Where local conditions create difficulties for the import of foreign products, export of knowhow or entering into a licensing or franchising agreement may be the one way of entering the market.

Having built the world's first steam locomotive in 1804, a prosperous period followed in the early part of the twentieth century, when British engineers built and operated steam railway systems around the world. With the passing of steam locomotives in favour of diesel or electric power, many highly qualified steam railway engineers were no longer required.

A country which still builds and operates steam locomotives is China, who now have the largest remaining factory building steam locomotives. China has ample supplies of labour and coal and can build steam locomotives for a fraction of the cost of diesels. To ensure availability of expert advice, China has offered consultancy work to a number of redundant engineers from British Rail's Doncaster works.

In order to overcome the problems of exporting to certain countries, there is a growing interest in countertrade; detailed below are some of the forms which this may take.

Barter is the least complicated form of countertrade, involving a straightforward exchange of goods.

Counter purchase is an arrangement where an exporter sells goods to an importer overseas for cash, and undertakes to use all or part of that money to purchase goods from the importer.

A further development is buyback or compensation trading. In this case an exporter of plant or machinery agrees to accept all or part of the payment in goods produced by that machinery.

Another variation is offset trading. In this type of operation, the exporter agrees with the importer that he will incorporate in his products materials, components or assemblies purchased from the importer. A variation on this theme is the example of Schweppes who wished to open up trade with Eastern Europe. In order to achieve this aim, it was agreed to accept payment in Bulgarian tomatoes. Schweppes then sold these to a subsidiary company in Sweden which manufactures tomato paste.

Where payment problems arise, a possible solution may be the use of an Escrow Trading Account. This is a form of agreement, where funds are delivered to a third party, and held pending completion of an agreement. In such a case, where an importer is unable to make immediate payment for goods, an agreement may be reached where payment to the exporter is made from the proceeds of the sale of the goods in question. In such an agreement, the goods are duly delivered to the importer, who then sells the goods, placing the proceeds in the agreed Escrow account. When sufficient funds have been built up in the Escrow account to pay the exporter, the payment is made from the Escrow account to the exporter to discharge the outstanding debt.

A more complicated form of countertrade is Switch Trading. It can happen that where two countries have a bilateral trade agreement, one country may build up a credit surplus with the other.

In such circumstances it may be possible to use the surplus funds to pay for imports from a third country. Brazil had a surplus in such an arrangement with Poland. It was therefore possible for Brazil to enter into a switch agreement with another country, paying with goods direct from Poland.

The growth of different types of countertrade has led to the appearance of specialist countertrade brokers. The United States Department of Commerce has predicted that by the end of the century, countertrade may account for as much as thirty per cent of world trade. This view is widely accepted in spite of the contrary opinion that the break up of the communist systems in Eastern Europe may bring a rapid reduction in countertrade.

Having considered a variety of sales organizations and options, mention must be made of a further invaluable aid to international trade, outward and inward missions.

Participation in outward missions will allow an exporter to explore the prospects for his goods or services. Newcomers to exporting will benefit from advice and assistance from other members of the group who may have had previous experience in the market. Travel grants are available from the Department of Trade and Industry's Overseas Promotion Support Branch (OPS) for missions sponsored by an approved trade association, chamber of commerce or other similar body.

In a similar manner, the Department of Trade and Industry's Inward Mission Scheme can provide help and financial support to bring groups of buyers, decision makers, and opinion formers to the United Kingdom to visit firms and promotional events.

Recruitment, Training and the Management of Sales Staff

In order to be successful in the field of export marketing, great care must be taken in the recruitment of sales staff.

Although there are inevitably similarities between the work of sales staff in the home market and those operating overseas, in that both are striving to achieve the same end result, the salesman overseas carries far more responsibilities than his counterpart in the home market. It is essential that a sales representative operating overseas has the knowledge and authority to make management decisions without having to consult his or her superior or head office. He or she will have a major responsibility in selecting and organizing the most appropriate channels of distribution as well as the appointment and supervision of agents and distributors – functions which would not be required of a home market salesman. An additional area of responsibility would be the organizing of advertising and exhibitions, and the possible negotiation of licensing agreements.

It is essential that an overseas sales representative should have both the knowledge and the authority to carry out these functions and, indeed, to act as the company in an overseas market. In the eyes of many customers he or she will be regarded as 'The Company'.

A very important aspect of an overseas sales representative's function is to undertake continuous market research, sending a constant flow of market information to head office.

A further important factor is the need to be totally fluent in the appropriate languages, always bearing in mind the level of linguistic ability which is required to conduct business in a foreign language.

As will be appreciated, many attributes are required of a successful export sales representative. In addition to any know-ledge and experience which newly appointed representatives have acquired in a previous job, they must undergo a period of well defined in-company training to ensure that not only do they have comprehensive product knowledge but also an in-depth knowledge of company methods and objectives.

Export of Capital Equipment

The problems faced by an exporter of capital equipment will be unlike those faced by exporters of consumer goods or services; consequently the initial approach to a market will be different.

One approach for the export of capital equipment, after having undertaken appropriate market research, is participation in an overseas trade fair which may well qualify for financial assistance from the Department of Trade and Industry.

Much capital equipment forms part of major international contracts such as contracts for railways, ports, airports, steel and chemical process plants, cable and telecommunications systems, irrigation and water supply projects, hospitals and universities.

The Projects and Export Policy division (PEP) of the

Department of Trade and Industry coordinates all government interests and support services for large overseas projects.

When exporting capital equipment, the project may well involve more than just the equipment, involving further responsibilities such as the installation and commissioning of plant together with the training of operatives. An important aspect of any such venture would be the provision of a total back up service to ensure adequate plant maintenance and the availability of spare parts.

Selection of an Overseas Agent

The selection and appointment of an overseas agent is of vital importance to an exporter. It is important to appreciate that in any market the agent may be the one contact which the exporter has with his customers.

Hence the wrong choice of an agent could have disastrous effects. When considering the appointment of an agent, several sources of help and information are available, for example, the Department of Trade and Industry, trade associations, chambers of commerce.

For most exporters, the choice will be a commission agent and the following questions should be put to potential candidates.

1 Is the agency a sole trader, partnership, limited company?
2 When was the agency founded?
3 Capitalization, names and holdings of partners or directors.
4 Names and ages of salesmen.
5 What other agencies are held?
6 May the other principals be contacted?
7 What is the turnover?
8 Average size of orders.
9 How many customers are regularly visited?
10 What forms of promotion are used? Cost?
11 What is the usual form of finance in trade?
12 What rate of commission is expected?
13 What showroom facilities are available?
14 Membership of trade associations or chambers of commerce.

15 Name of bankers.
16 Any other essential information.

It will be helpful if it is possible to appoint an agent who has previous experience with your type of products, and who does not already represent any competitive interests.

In many instances, a commission agent will represent more than one company. The important thing to ensure is that an agent does not carry too many lines to be able to devote the fullest attention to your products. However, there may be instances where it will be helpful for an agent to handle complementary lines, as this may help to provide an entry to new outlets.

It should be understood that the general term agent has a variety of meanings, although the most commonly used form is a commission agent, whose only remuneration will be a commission on sales.

When selecting an agent, the exporter must look not merely for the elementary trading virtues like honesty and solvency, nor confine himself to checking the physical equipment needed for getting the goods to the customer. The prudent exporter will appoint a commission agent who is steeped in what can only be described as the social culture of his market, and that is not merely a matter of language, nor does it stop at religion, it embraces an entire way of life which forms the consumer matrix into which the exporter's goods must fit. Needless to say, the best agents will be cosmopolitans, at home in at least two worlds – those of the producer and the consumer. To describe one such would be to paint a picture of a paragon but the exporter should seek evidence, not merely verbal assurances, of skill in promoting the sales of products bearing at least some resemblance to its own.

It is incorrect to expect that an overseas agent merely requires a price list and a range of samples to ensure success in its market, no matter how great the merits of the product concerned.

Following the selection an agent must be thoroughly briefed by the exporter. Indeed it should be a two-way briefing: an outward briefing of the properties, uses and maintenance of the product, and an inward briefing covering every facet of the market that the exporter needs to know about.

The general term agent may of course refer to a one-person operation or a large well-organized undertaking. Both types can be effective, but in the case of the smaller organization, an important aspect to be considered is the prospect of continuity.

Ideally, the appointment of an agent will result from a visit to the selected agent company on its home territory; wherever possible a newly appointed agent should be brought to the United Kingdom as an essential element in its briefing on the principal's background, policies and above all the products. In order to operate effectively, an agent must never be regarded as merely a name on an agreement or organization chart. It should be regarded as a vitally important part of the organization, equal in importance to the exporters' head office marketing staff. In the eyes of many overseas customers who may never have any direct contact with the exporter's home-based staff it must be stressed again that the agent will be regarded as the company. In order to present the correct image, it must be advised on the current position regarding production, deliveries, prices and many other details of the business. In fact a constant flow of information between the agent and the exporter represent essential ingredients for a satisfactory agency arrangement.

Agreement for an Overseas Commission Agent

Having decided to appoint a commission agent overseas, the first essential is to draw up a mutually acceptable agency agreement. Such an agreement will usually be for an initial trial period, maybe for twelve months, to be mutually reviewed in the light of experience during the trial period. When drawing up an agreement it is vital to define very clearly the level of authority which will be delegated to the agent.

Essentially an agency agreement is a contract between an exporter and an agent, which is drawn up with the intention of: clarifying the aims and intentions of the parties; recording the headings of agreement; providing an agreed document of reference, in case of dispute; and establishing a means of complying with the formalities of documentation, financing, exchange and trade control at home and abroad.

Any agency agreement should be drawn up by legal advisers. In some instances the exporter may have a standard agreement which can be amended to meet the needs of individual markets.

When no formal agreement has been entered into and a dispute arises, the courts will endeavour to determine the intentions of the parties from the evidence which they may give according due weight to any correspondence which has passed between them.

The majority of the clauses which follow are normally common to any agency agreement for a commission agent. They may, however, be amended in order to meet the special needs of each case.

1   The names of the parties to the agreement, together with the registered addresses.

2   The purpose of the contract, stating in specific terms that A appoints B as a commission agent, and that B agrees to act in that capacity, subject to the terms outlined in the following clauses.

3   A description of the products or services covered by the agreement which the exporter will offer for sale and the agent agrees to sell, including a reference to any brand names.

4   A precise description of the territory to be covered by the agent, having exclusive rights in the prescribed territory. Division may be made by political or geographic divisions. For example, a specified country, or alternatively, specified zones within that country.

5   The duties of the principal, covering reference to sales outside the agency, and the handling of direct enquiries.

6   The duties of the agent. Arrangements for dealing with any other suppliers.

7 Details of any exceptions, reserves or restrictions.

8 The method of quoting prices, for example Free on Board (FOB) or any other method.

9 Purchase and re-sale by the agent. If the agent is allowed to purchase on its own account and act as a distributor, in addition to its functions as a commission agent; whether or not it will be allowed to appoint sub-distributors subject to the exporter's approval, fix resale prices and retail list prices and report back to the manufacturer.
In addition, the agent may place orders with the manufacturer for direct supply to the buyers, with an agreed percentage to be paid to the agent. The contact must also establish: whether or not commission is to be paid on orders not placed through the agent but originating from within the agreed territory; whether the agent is to assume del credere services (including the provision of credit) on its orders; and whether any consignment trade is contemplated, if so fixing responsibility for price determination.

10 General arrangements for types of sales contracts such as free on board (FOB), cost, insurance and freight (CIF) for giving shipping instructions, arranging insurance and related matters.

11 For any consignments made under clauses 9 and 10, it will be necessary to establish the following: how the goods are to be delivered; who pays landing charges, duty, customs clearance, cartage, porterage, warehousing, insurance in warehouse and accounting arrangements; and property in goods, arrangements for release to buyers, disposal of stock on termination of agreement.

12 Spares, for general maintenance and service, together with arrangements for disposal on termination of agreement.

13 Responsibility for payment for cables, air mails or any similar additional expenses.

14 Responsibility of the principal where force majeure prevents delivery from factory, or prevents dispatch, or

causes diversion of ship or plane.

15 A permissive clause where the products do not meet the competition in styling, suitability for market or price, whether or not the agent is allowed to handle other goods in the same category. This agent's permissive clause is more common in the case of a commission agent than with a sole distributor.

16 To determine an agreed rate of commission, either on a fixed rate or a sliding scale. How commission is to be paid or credited.

17 Requirement for the agent to keep proper books and render periodical statements, including consignment stocks where applicable. Books to be subject to inspection by exporter, or by someone authorized by the exporter.

18 Publicity: general agreement regarding sales literature and catalogues including responsibility for any necessary translations; policy on exhibitions, local advertising and any special promotions; agreement regarding allocation of costs or, in case of agreement to share, allocation of shares between parties.

19 Agent to submit reports at agreed times. Principal to keep agent advised concerning product development and general trade. Also on manufacturing and marketing policy.

20 General conditions not already mentioned, such as that the agent is not to pledge principal's credit or to commence legal proceeding without his approval.

21 Time for which the agreement is to run without notice, together with period of notice thereafter. How any notice is to be given and whether both parties have reciprocal rights on the same terms.

22 Arrangements for a summary determination in case of breach or default by either party or upon liquidation.

23 As the agreement will usually be between parties in different countries, it is important to establish which laws will apply in the case of any dispute.

24 Neither party has the right to assign the benefits of the contract without the prior written consent of the other.

The agreement should be signed by both parties, with an indication of the capacity of the signatories, and witnesses, including application of the company's seal, where applicable.

As previously mentioned, these clauses will normally have to be considered when drawing up any agency agreement. However, with the creation of the Single European Market, a new European Community Directive on agents has been drawn up. In accordance with European Community Law, the United Kingdom was due to implement EC Directive 86/653 on 1 January 1994.

This Directive will make a number of significant changes in the law governing agents and will enhance the rights of an agent against a principal. It is most important that anyone who has agency arrangements in Europe, should acquaint themselves with the new regulations and tailor their agency agreements and arrangements to comply with the new law.

In addition to concluding agreements for commission agents, it may sometimes be necessary to enter into slightly different contracts to cover, for example, the following: agreement between an exporter and a sole distributor in an overseas market; appointment of a commission agent to handle sales to buyers for direct shipment to them and for release from consignment stock; agreement between a United Kingdom manufacturer and a United Kingdom-based merchant, having a well-establish branch in an overseas country through which sales and deliveries may be channelled.

Specimen Agreements

Detailed below are examples of suitable forms of agreement to cover the above mentioned situations. It should be remembered, when studying these specimen agreements, that they are given as general examples only. In many countries the requirements of binding agreements are specific to that country and special care must be taken to ensure that such requirements are satisfied.

Contract between exporter and distributor

1 Memorandum of Agreement made this ....
day of .... 19...... between XY Manufacturing
Co Ltd, whose registered address is ....
....
(hereinafter called XYM) and .... (hereinafter
called the distributor) whereby it is agreed that:

2 XYM appoints the distributor as and from the date of this
agreement to be the sole distributor, and the distributor
agrees to act as such to establish and promote sales

3 of XYM products, supplied by XYM under that brand name
(hereinafter called the products) and to refrain from selling
or factoring or otherwise collaborating in the sale of
products competing with or in the same class of merchandise as the products of XYM

4 in the territory agreed upon and XYM agrees not to sell to
others in the territory or to sell to others for re-sale in the
territory.

5 XYM agrees to supply to the distributor such reasonable and
adequate supplies of the products as shall be ordered by the
distributor subject to confirmation of such orders by D. Ltd
whose registered address is .... as buyer's agent
and shipper except in the case of orders received from
shippers on behalf of other importers where the shipper
shall prove acceptable to XYM and acceptance of the order
shall be authorized by the distributor and the price subject
to commission at the rate of five per cent on the FOB price,
such commission being payable to the distributor upon
settlement of the account. XYM agrees to refer to the
distributor all enquiries for the products received from the
territory.

6 The distributor agrees not to bind the credit of XYM in any
way and not so to act as to compromise the credit of XYM
and to undertake no guarantee or warranty in respect of the
products except as shall previously have been authorized by
XYM in writing and in all matters of trade or technical

description shall faithfully follow such description as shall be established or ratified by XYM in relation to suitability for use of the products in the territory.

7 XYM reserves the right to enter upon manufacture of any products whatsoever under brand names other than XYM without consulting the distributor or remunerating the distributor in any way for any such products which may be sold in the territory.

8 XYM shall quote all prices to the distributor at its best FOB terms.

9 The distributor agrees to instruct its buying agent herein-before named to accept the products so delivered upon ocean vessel nominated by the said buying agent for insured transit to the territory. The distributor agrees to construct a schedule of cost, insurance, freight, landed duty paid prices, re-sale prices to retail traders and fixed retail prices for sale to the public at the hands of retailers for ratification by XYM. The distributor shall have the right to appoint retail traders for the sale of the products in the territory and shall authorize them to hold out as authorized dealers in the product, provided, however, that if complaints shall reach XYM from the territory in respect of the conduct of such retail traders XYM shall have the right to require that the distributor take all necessary steps to rescind the authorized dealer appointment of the offending party.

10 XYM shall cause to be prepared a standard spares list not exceeding two per cent by value of the products. The distributor shall purchase import stock and maintain such stocks of spares according to list. Upon determination of this agreement all stocks of spares held by the distributor shall be held at the disposal of XYM and disposed of as XYM may at that time direct.

11 XYM agrees to meet all costs of cables and mail charges on messages to the territory. The distributor agrees to pay all cable and postal charges which may reasonably be incurred in communicating with XYM.

12 In the event of delivery being frustrated or delayed by strikes, riots, lockouts, trade disputes, acts of restraint by kings, princes or governors or other cause not within the control of XYM then XYM is held absolved of all loss of trade or profit consequent upon such cause.

13 Where it shall be proved to the reasonable satisfaction of XYM that the products are not competitive with other similar merchandise in the territory, then the distributor shall be at liberty to engage upon the sale of similar products obtained from other suppliers.

14 The distributor shall claim upon XYM quarterly on the last days of March, June, September and December in respect of all commissions payable under clause 5 and publicity disbursements under clause 16 hereof and shall

15 at all times keep and maintain proper books of account in respect of his purchases and sales of the products and dealings in relation thereto.

16 XYM agrees to provide free of charge sales leaflets, sales aids and service manuals in English in reasonable quantities. The distributor shall submit his local publicity scheme half-yearly in advance for ratification by XYM and XYM shall reimburse the distributor half-yearly in arrears and after receipt of receipted invoices for one half of such publicity disbursements provided however that XYM's liability hereunder shall in no case exceed two and one half per cent of Free on Board turnover during the same half year.

17 The distributor shall report in writing to XYM within one month of the completion of each half year upon the conduct and development of business in the products during the period and generally upon trade conditions in the territory.

18 The distributor shall not without prior knowledge and consent of XYM pledge the credit of XYM.

19 This agreement shall continue for two calendar years from the date hereof and thereafter for six months from the date of the giving of notice in writing by either party to the other.

The distributor shall send notice by registered post to the registered address of XYM and notice by XYM shall be sent to the last known address of the distributor.

20 This agreement shall be summarily determined in the case of breach of any clause hereof or in the event of liquidation whether forced or voluntary.

21 In all disputes upon the interpretation of this agreement the law of England shall apply.

22 The benefits of this agreement shall under no circumstances be assignable.

As witness our hands etc........

Contract between principal and commission agent

1 Memorandum of agreement made this .... day of .... 19.... between XY Manufacturing Co Ltd whose registered address is .... in the county of .... (hereinafter called the Principal) and A.................... and B................. Ltd, of .... (hereinafter called the Agent) whereby it is agreed that:

2 The Principal appoints the Agent to be his sole agent as and from the date of this agreement and the Agent agrees diligently to serve the Principal by all means to promote and extend the sale of

3 .... products manufactured in England or elsewhere by or for the Principal (hereinafter called the products) and the Agent undertakes not so to act as to prevent the sale of the products or interfere with the development of the Principal's trade or to buy, sell or deal in any way with products which the Principal may claim to constitute competition with the products in .... (hereinafter called the territory).

4 The Principal agrees not to supply the products to any party located within the territory or to any party not being so located who is known to intend resale in the territory except where the related order shall have reached the Principal (a) from the Agent by mail or cable, (b) direct from a party nominated by the Agent, (c) direct from a party not previously nominated but who shall upon reference to the agent prove to be acceptable to him.

5   The Agent agrees not to bind the credit of the Principal in any way and not so to act as to compromise the credit of the Principal and to undertake no guarantee or warranty in respect of the products except as shall previously have been authorized by the Principal in writing and in all matters of trade or technical description shall follow such description as shall be established or ratified by the Principal in relation to suitability for use of the products in the territory.

6   The Principal shall have the right to continue to sell and supply the products to the companies named on list in Appendix A to this agreement without accounting to the Agent in any way, such sales lying entirely outside the terms of this agreement.

7   The Principal shall quote all prices CIF to ports in the territory.

8   In every case of orders placed by the Agent, the Principal shall reserve a commission of five per cent for the Agent calculated on FOB prices, free of special export packing stipulated by the buyer. In every other case of orders placed with the Principal within the terms of clause 5 of this agreement the Principal shall reserve a commission for the Agent of six per cent calculated on FOB value net of special export packing, such commission being in remuneration of the sales promotion activities of the Agent. And it is further agreed that in every order placed by the Agent he shall indicate that he acts del credere and authorizes the principal to incorporate his name as case of need upon the bill of exchange drawn upon the buyer to finance the related transaction. Upon all other transactions not being the subject of orders placed by the Agent no del credere function or responsibility attaches to him and

the Principal agrees upon all such orders to require of the buyer that he provide finance by irrevocable letter of credit confirmed by London bankers.

The Principal agrees to credit the Agent with del credere commission calculated at two per cent on the CIF price of all the products sold to buyers in respect of whom the Agent has accepted del credere risk as provided herein.

All commissions the subject of this clause are considered to have been earned when effective payment has reached the Principal. Commission account is agreed to be transferable quarterly commencing 31 March 19.... without loss of exchange for the agent and the Principal shall arrange for the transfer of sums due and payable hereunder through banks or bankers whose charges shall be payable by the Principal.

9   In respect of new lines launched in future by the Principal it is agreed that the Principal shall provide and ship consignment stocks to the territory at his own responsibility and expense. Such consignment stocks shall be held at a mutually agreed place to order of the Principal for release to buyers against delivery orders signed by the Principal and countersigned by the Agent. In support of consignment sales, the Principal shall provide free samples and ship them at his own expense to the Agent in advance of shipment of consignment stocks.

10 The Agent shall purchase the trade periodicals listed in Appendix B to this agreement and shall apply suitable markings to such passages therein as his knowledge of the trade and the territory shall lead him to regard as important information for the Principal.

The Agent shall faithfully record costs incurred hereunder: together with all costs of cables incurred in connection with its communications with the Principal, which costs shall be charged as to one half to the Principal, the remaining half being borne by the Agent.

11 The Agent agrees that in the event of frustration or delayed

delivery no cause of claim or action shall arise on the agent's part as against the Principal.

12 Commissions payable under clause 8 and expenses payable under clause 10 hereof shall be payable quarterly upon claim by the Agent to which end he shall maintain proper books of account open at reasonable time to inspection by or under authority of the Principal.

13 The Agent shall have the right at his absolute discretion to quote prices in excess of the CIF price given to him by the Principal as laid down in clause 8 and upon payment for deliveries at over price shall be entitled to one half of such over price.

14 The Agent shall submit suitable publicity schemes for advertisements in the territory and shall place contracts for such advertisements on behalf of the Principal as he shall deem to be reasonable.

15 The Agent shall report in writing to the Principal within one month of the end of every half year upon the conduct and development of business in the products during the period and generally upon trade conditions in the territory with his reasoned views on the immediate prospects.

16 The Agent shall describe himself as Agent for the Principal but shall at no time hold out to have the right to pledge the credit of the Principal except as provided by this agreement or unless he shall first have obtained the consent of the Principal in writing.

17 This agreement shall remain in force for one year from date hereof and thereafter for three months from notice to determine being delivered by registered post by either party to the other.

18 The Principal shall have the right to determine this agreement without notice in the event of the breach of any provision hereof by the agent or upon forced sale of his assets, seizure of his effects under legal process or upon his insolvency.

19 The Agent shall not, without prior written consent of the Principal attempt to assign the benefits of this agreement and the Principal shall have the right of summary determination in the event of such attempt being proved to his reasonable satisfaction.

20 This agreement shall be interpreted according to the law in force in England, and any process hereupon shall be undertaken in English courts.

As witness our hands etc.................

Contract between manufacturer and merchant

1 Memorandum of agreement made this .... day of .... 19.... between XYM Ltd whose registered address is .... (hereinafter called the Manufacturers) and GH Marketing Ltd whose registered address is .... (hereinafter called the Merchant) whereby it is agreed that:

2 The Manufacturers appoint the Merchant to be their sole representative as and from the date of this agreement and until determined as hereinafter provided

3 of all the merchandise manufactured by the Manufacturers (hereinafter called the products)

4 for sale in or supply to Venezuela (hereinafter referred to as the agency territory)

5 which shall be supplied to the Merchant in England for resale through their branches in Venezuela within the terms hereinafter provided. The Manufacturers shall take no action upon enquiries received from or for shipment to the agency territory but shall refer them immediately to the Merchant.

6 The Merchant agrees not to bind the credit of the manufacturers and so to act as not to compromise the credit of the Manufacturers and to undertake no guarantee or warranty in respect of the products except as shall previously have been authorized by the Manufacturers in writing and in all matters of trade or technical description shall faithfully follow such description as shall be established or ratified by the Manufacturers in relation to the products with especial reference to suitability for use in the territory.

7   The Manufacturers shall quote all prices ex factory but upon the request of the Merchant shall nevertheless be prepared at all reasonable times to convey and deliver the products by its own transport or by public conveyance to such port or ports or other destination in Great Britain as shall be nominated by the Merchant for a consideration agreed upon audit by or for the parties hereto to constitute a true net cost of such transport service and related insurance upon terms usual in the trade.

8   The Merchant agrees to place acceptable orders with the Manufacturers for a minimum total of ten thousand pounds in every calendar year during which this agreement shall remain in force, such order to be acknowledged by the Manufacturers in indication of acceptance. Orders hereunder shall be placed with and accepted by the Manufacturers not less than six weeks before delivery is required by the Merchant.

9   The Merchant shall at all times keep the Manufacturers advised of conditions in the agency territory and of developments offering opportunity for increased turnover and in particular it is agreed that the Merchant shall upon signature of this agreement cause to be instituted a market research exercise in the agency territory to determine whether or not the establishment of consignment stocks in depot would yield advantages. In the event of consignment stocks being ordered it is agreed that they will not exceed ten thousand pounds at FOB values, and that all costs and disbursements upon and after shipment shall be borne by the Merchant, that accounts of sales and payment therefore shall be tendered to the Manufacturers quarterly commencing three calendar months after the date of loading on ship of the first consignment order. The property in such

consignment stock remains in the Manufacturers, and the Merchant agrees to transfer physical possession to the Manufacturers or their nominee upon request in writing or upon the expiry of notice to determine this agreement.

10 Where any cause outside the control of the Manufacturers shall lead to non delivery or late delivery the minimum quantity of clause 8 shall upon claim by the Merchant be proportionately reduced without giving ground for determination of this agreement but except for this reduction the Merchant agrees to make no claim for loss or damage consequent upon such delay or non delivery.

11 This agreement shall remain in force for five years from date hereof except in the case of notice being given by one party to the other at the registered address in writing when unless the parties shall otherwise agree six months notice shall be required before effective determination.

12 Notice under clause 11 shall be excused and the agreement summarily determined upon winding-up, liquidation or assignment of assets by either party or if without prior agreement in writing of the other party, either shall merge, come under control of or amalgamate with another company.

13 Disputes upon the interpretation of the whole or any part of this agreement shall be referred to an arbitrator to be appointed by the London Chamber of Commerce and the parties agree to state their cases to such arbitrator and bind themselves to accept his decision.

As witness to our hands etc............

It should be stressed that the foregoing examples are designed to illustrate the types of agreements which may have to be concluded to undertake overseas trade. However, it is important to remember that, as in the case of the European Community previously mentioned, many countries have their own legal requirements for forms of agreement. It is therefore of vital importance to investigate fully the legal position in each market where it is proposed to enter into such an agreement.

Questions for Discussion

1 Describe how you would make a sales forecast.

2 State what you understand by *Incoterms*; give four examples.

3 List any ten questions which you would put to a candidate for appointment as an overseas agent.

7

Communication

Internal Communication

When considering the question of communication, it is easy to think in terms of the obvious areas such as sales promotion, publicity and public relations, all of which play an important role in the general field of communication. Later in this chapter detailed attention will be paid to advertising which is a vital factor in the overall communication process.

However, it must be appreciated that the whole question of communication must start within the company itself. It is vital that staff at all levels throughout the company be totally aware of the aims and objectives which the company hopes to achieve in the export field.

This means that every effort must be made to ensure that each department within a company be made aware of and be involved in the export effort. Initially, research and development and also design personnel must be involved to ensure that they make every possible effort to meet the precise needs of customers overseas.

An important element is the total involvement of the production departments to ensure, first and foremost, that they are able to produce exactly what the markets require. Above all production departments must be fully aware of the need to meet delivery dates on time. It cannot be over-emphasized that one of the easiest ways to lose customers' goodwill is when delivery promises are not met.

The finance department must be involved throughout, in order to be aware of all the possible financial problems which may have to be overcome.

Departments concerned with selling, distribution and, where appropriate, after sales service must be involved at all times in the company's marketing plans to ensure that they are fully aware of all the possible problems which may arise, and to ensure that they are in a position to make the maximum contribution to meeting the company's export aims.

The importance of total communication within a company cannot be over-emphasized. In this context consideration might be given to organizing an inward mission by overseas visitors to the company, as this would provide an excellent opportunity of establishing face-to-face contact between a range of factory staff and potential overseas customers. Such personal contacts frequently enhance the chances of establishing good business relationships with overseas contacts.

The Department of Trade and Industry will provide assistance to participants in inward missions where they are sponsored by an approved trade association or similar body. The Department's inward missions scheme will provide financial assistance towards the cost of travel to the United Kingdom, accommodation, meals and also a suitable reception.

Advertising

Advertising is the purchase of space in a chosen medium.

Before undertaking an advertising campaign, consideration must be given to the wide range of media which is available. The choice of the most appropriate medium will vary both in accordance with the product and also the media available in the chosen market.

For a range of consumer products, there will usually be a number of available options such as newspapers, magazines, radio and television.

In the case of industrial products the emphasis will frequently be on technical journals, or possibly the use of film or video presentations to specialist audiences.

When organizing an overseas advertising campaign, great care must be taken in the selection of appropriate media, and a decision must be made as to whether the services of a specialist advertising agency are appropriate. In many overseas markets the available range of media will be entirely different from the options available in the United Kingdom. National newspapers do not exist in all overseas markets and greater use has to be made of other options including local newspapers and radio stations. In addition to considering the types of media available in a market, it will be evident that the final choice will also be governed by the type of product or services which you wish to advertise. An example of this is a range of technical or industrial goods and services where any advertising campaign would be undertaken in specialist journals.

In the United Kingdom we are accustomed to having a wide range of media from which to make our choice, but in the case of some overseas markets it may be necessary to consider other options such as billboards or local cinema advertising.

It is most important to undertake detailed research before embarking on an advertising campaign in order to ascertain if any special restrictions apply in a particular market. Just as in the home market where there are restrictions on the advertising of cigarettes, many overseas markets have their own restrictions on what advertising material may be used and these must be fully investigated. In France, for example, restrictions are placed on the size of outside advertising displays and in Germany there are strict controls governing claims which may be made for a product advertised. The entire approach to advertising in an overseas market may be different from accepted practice in the home market.

In certain countries, for example in many Middle Eastern countries, it should be remembered that many types of advertising are unacceptable. For instance, different colours have different meanings and care must be taken not to use colour schemes which may be considered offensive. In Europe white signifies purity and elegance, in many Far Eastern countries this colour denotes death or mourning. In addition it is important to ensure that your advertising material will not offend any religious beliefs. Similarly in these markets it would be inappropriate to feature pictures of scantily clad women, which may be perfectly acceptable in the United Kingdom but which would be considered most offensive in some countries. A drinks company once discovered that such pictures reversed the intended message by saying: 'nice women do not go for this drink'.

The answers to these problems must be found by undertaking suitable market research before embarking on an advertising campaign.

It should also be remembered that an advertising campaign will almost certainly cover a number of advertisements possibly using a variety of media as it is unlikely that a 'one-off' advertisement will make a lasting impact.

A vital factor when considering the choice of media is the cost involved. In the home market we are accustomed to seeing an enormous amount of advertising making use of media such as television, national newspapers, magazines and radio. When considering the most appropriate medium for your advertising, cost will be of paramount importance. Initially it will be necessary to establish a target sales figure for a market, in order to be in a position to establish an advertising budget which will almost certainly be geared to anticipated sales in the market. In this context savings can frequently be made by placing a series of advertisements which will normally offer cost savings when compared with the cost of a single advertisement.

In many instances, especially in the case of smaller companies, advertising programmes may be limited by lack of finance. Nevertheless it is important to be aware of and to consider all the available options.

Advertising should be selective, and it is important to undertake research in order to be able to plan the use of media which will be most appropriate to reach your target audience. It is obvious that you would be unlikely to consider advertising cosmetics in an engineering journal, nevertheless it must be emphasized that whatever type of product or service you wish to advertise, it is vitally important to place your advertisements in the most appropriate medium, depending on the product or service to be advertised. It is important to consider all available media. In addition to the possible choice of television or radio, not only daily newspapers may be considered but also the available range of weekly or monthly publications. In some cases the product or service may make technical or specialist journals the obvious choice.

If there is a need to consider an advertising campaign in a third world country, it will be necessary to forget the traditional media to which we are accustomed in the home market, and investigate a range of other options such as advertising on buses, hoardings or cinema screens. In such cases extensive text would be inappropriate and the emphasis would be on pictorial presentation.

When planning an advertising campaign, the following possible objectives must be taken into consideration:

1 the need to create an interest and awareness of a product in a market;
2 the possibilities of selling a new product in an established market;
3 the ways in which it may be possible to support and promote the sale of existing products or services in an existing market.

It will be appreciated that the approach required to achieve these objectives may be quite different in each market.

In addition to setting objectives it is important to consider aspects such as competitive strategies, characteristics, atmosphere and above all budgetary control.

Working with Own Sales Staff

A number of basic facts must be established before it will be possible to decide on an advertising campaign.

Initially, it will be important to clarify the company's aims, policies and strategies. In other words, to establish the company's short-and long-term aims, in terms of image, products or services to be advertised, also the company's policies to attain these aims. It will be important to devise a strategy for individual products in terms of image, target audience, position in the market, also the projected product life cycle.

Consideration must be given to the functions which must be performed to ensure that the advertising emphasises the brand strategy which has been selected. A further important factor is to consider what parts of an advertising campaign can be carried out in-company, and in what areas it may be necessary to enlist the help of outside agencies.

A further important factor to consider is the availability of suitably qualified staff to carry out these functions.

It may be necessary to initiate a programme of staff training, to ensure the availability of staff with adequate knowledge and skills to devise and manage an effective advertising campaign.

Before devising an advertising programme for a product it will be important to consider the stage which has been reached in the product life cycle, also the product's position in the company's product mix.

A detailed study must be made of the markets to be targeted in an advertising campaign. Due consideration must be given to the economic situation in a market and the potential customers to be targeted. In addition it will be important to study trends in the market and carry out a thorough investigation of potential outlets and their location.

A study must be made of the available media in a market, considering relative strengths and weaknesses, in terms of performance, colour and cost effectiveness.

A matter of major importance will be to determine the procedures to be followed to evaluate the results of a campaign.

It will be necessary to draw up an advertising brief, and to ensure that staff involved are able to communicate clearly both in writing, verbally and visually.

A further matter of importance will be to establish what will be the relationship between the advertising manager the brand manager and other managers within the company.

Where a company has established a presence in a market overseas, possibly by appointing a resident agent or even setting up an overseas subsidiary, it may well be possible to mount an advertising campaign without making use of the services of a professional agency.

However, this will only be possible where a company has its own organization established in the overseas market, having not only qualified staff capable of mounting and managing an advertising campaign, but above all a detailed knowledge of local conditions and needs.

Working with United Kingdom based Advertising Agencies

Advertising is not only highly specialized but also highly organized, and it is important to appreciate that it may be necessary to enlist the services of a professional advertising agency.

In considering the use of an advertising agency, it is important to investigate and evaluate the agency's previous experience and performance in the market selected.

Much useful guidance on the choice of an advertising agency may be obtained from sources such as the Department of Trade and Industry, trade associations, chambers of commerce and banks.

A growing number of United Kingdom based advertising agencies now have overseas subsidiaries or associates who are able to provide invaluable assistance in mounting an advertising campaign in an overseas market.

In order to exploit the possibilities of exporting their products to Eastern Europe, Mars Confectionery of Slough resolved to mount an advertising campaign in Moscow and St Petersburg. They enlisted the services of Darcy, Masius Benton & Bowles to initiate an intensive television advertising campaign in these cities for their Snickers bars. In addition to the advertising campaign Mars resolved to sponsor Russia's football team, with 'Snickers' emblazoned across their shirts.

Although Snickers are priced at the equivalent of seventeen pence, in a country where the average monthly wage is only £15 the level of sales generated by the campaign was remarkable, the distributors claiming that they can sell twenty containers full of Snickers every day in Moscow alone.

An essential element of an advertising campaign is to capture the attention of the public, and of course generate public support and sales.

In 1987 Gold Blend freeze dried coffee launched an advertising campaign which almost developed into a soap opera, running to no less than eleven episodes. The company now claims that the campaign has become one of the country's most successful advertising campaigns. In terms of attracting public interest, this was so successful that the romantic novelist Suzannah James wrote a 345 page novel, 'Love over Gold' based on the activities of the couple featured in the advertisements.

As a result of this campaign, the sales of Gold Blend coffee increased by forty per cent, representing the equivalent of eleven million more cups a day, to make the product the most popular freeze dried coffee in the country.

Working with an Overseas Advertising Agency

Whether working with a United Kingdom based advertising agency, or one based overseas the arrangement will ensure the availability of the necessary specialized knowledge of the overseas market, and make available advice on the most appropriate media in the market concerned. As will be readily appreciated it would be extremely unlikely that an exporter would be able to obtain such information and expertise without help from a professional advertising agency.

In addition to providing guidance on the selection of media, an arrangement with an overseas based advertising agency would be able to provide an opportunity for discussing and planning a suitable campaign to meet the special needs of the chosen market. In addition it would provide the exporter with guidance on the most appropriate way in which to produce a full range of additional advertising material such as brochures, illustrated catalogues and other appropriate literature in the language of the overseas market. Access to local knowledge would be essential to succeed in producing the right material for a given market.

When working with an advertising agency, it is important not only to discuss and decide on a suitable advertising campaign, but above all to pay particular attention to the control of costs and the establishment of a suitable method of evaluating the results of the campaign.

It is unlikely that a campaign can be used without alteration in a number of different markets. Consideration must always be given to creating the right characteristics in a campaign to ensure acceptance in a given market.

Before embarking on an advertising campaign organized by an overseas agency, it must be appreciated that in many markets specialist agencies such as those available in the United Kingdom do not exist. As a result the greatest care has to be taken before entering into an agreement with an agency based overseas to establish exactly what experience they have and to investigate fully their ability to undertake a successful campaign.

Before entering into any agreement it is important to ensure that you will be able to control and evaluate the agency's performance as this will obviously be more difficult than would be the case with a home based agency.

The Importance of Foreign Language Material

Reference has already been made to the vital importance of obtaining suitable translations of material for use in an overseas market.

Each language has its own idioms and colloquialisms and these must be studied in detail and fully understood. A literal translation of an English text will often result in a total loss of impact or, even more importantly, a total distortion of the original message. For this reason special attention is required if it is intended to adapt an advertising campaign for use in different overseas markets.

Initially translations should be undertaken by a native speaker of the target market. In view of the many differences in the use of words and especially technical terms in different countries it is important that even translations undertaken by a native speaker should be submitted for final approval to a resident agent or distributor, or even a customer, in the target market.

The problem is well illustrated by the experience of the Esso Petroleum Company in the nineteen sixties. Having had considerable success with the 'Put a tiger in your tank' campaign, it was resolved to use this on a worldwide basis. This is where the problems began. It was soon apparent that a literal translation would be impossible because the literal translation of 'tank' would not convey the desired message in certain countries. After undertaking considerable research it was decided that the problem might be resolved by substituting words such as 'car' or 'engine'. Even this did not solve all the problems due to variations in the meaning of a word in different countries despite the fact that countries may have a common language.

For example, in Germany the Esso slogan became 'Pack Den Tiger in Den Tank' but in Switzerland and Austria the translation was 'Tu Den Tiger in Den Tank.'

A more recent example of the perils of translation was the experience of the Vauxhall Motor Company who had to change the name of their 'Nova' model in Spanish speaking countries as in Spanish the word translates as 'Does not go' – hardly an appropriate name for a car.

Questions for Discussion

1 State what you understand by internal communication within a company. Why is this important?

2 Describe your understanding of the term 'advertising'.

3 Give examples of factors to be considered when using foreign language material in advertising.

8

Political and Legal Constraints

Economic, Political and Legal Constraints

In many overseas markets it will be necessary to consider a range of uncontrollable variables which are sometimes referred to as PEST – Political, Economic, Social and Technological.

It is most important to investigate any restrictions which may be applied to imports in an overseas market. There will frequently be hurdles to overcome which do not exist in the home market.

International marketing requires a comprehensive understanding of the conditions under which it will be necessary to operate in an overseas market, which may fall under any of the above mentioned variables. Obviously having identified any such problems, steps must be undertaken to overcome them.

In order to investigate and resolve problems about import restrictions in an overseas market, an invaluable source of information is the Department of Trade and Industry (DTI).

The DTI operates specialized country desks dealing exclusively with individual markets. The Department's country desk officers work closely with the Foreign and Commonwealth Office commercial staff overseas and can provide a wide range of useful information on the following:

1 the political and economic situation,
2 local business conditions,
3 market prospects and product suitability,
4 local tariffs and other import regulations,
5 business contacts,
6 doing business in the market.

Much relevant information is available in the United Kingdom. Should the information required not be available, the country desk officer or your local regional office can contact commercial experts overseas and commission on behalf of the exporter a chargeable tailor-made export service.

The available range of services is described fully in the Department of Trade and Industry brochure 'Specific Export Help'. This invaluable publication contains details of how the DTI and commercial staff at diplomatic service posts overseas can help to obtain advice about the prospects for your products in the overseas markets in which you are interested.

In some markets, cargo delivery laws may be imposed. An example of this restriction on trade would be a case where the importer buys goods on an ex-works basis, and assumes responsibility for all freight and insurance charges. In many cases the country of the importer will insist that freight be carried by their own national carrier. The object of this legislation is to help preserve foreign currency, by insisting that the importer makes all the necessary arrangements for freight and insurance using the country's own currency. This requirement is on the increase and frequently forms part of bilateral or multilateral trade agreements.

The above illustrates some of the differences in marketing techniques in the Western bloc countries, Eastern bloc states and third world countries. Comparison should be made with the relatively buoyant economies such as are found in some European and North American countries.

As in the United Kingdom, a number of voluntary codes of practice and conduct exist in overseas markets. Examples of such codes of practice in the United Kingdom are the British Code of Advertising Practice, and the Market Research Society Code of Conduct. In the United Kingdom various legislation exists to protect consumer interests. Details of these and other legal and ethical constraints to international marketing may be found in a variety of market reports issued by international banks such as Barclays, Midland, National Westminster and Lloyds. In addition, valuable information appears in the publications of the Department of Trade and Industry. The valuable reports produced by the international banks are available free on request.

In addition to any legal and ethical constraints, there may well be non-economic objectives. Obviously a most important objective is profitability, but it will frequently be accompanied by others; for example, a company may wish to be:

- the leader in its field for innovation,
- the leader in its field for quality,
- the leader in its field for financial security,
- the leader in its field for safety,
- the leader in its field for reliability.

Even where the key economic objective is an adequate long-term return on resources, a company will frequently be influenced by these non-economic objectives.

Some business organizations are notably philanthropic and support foundations and trusts for the benefit of medicine, education and international understanding. Some pursue reasonably dedicated profitability but declare that all personnel have secure employment and that promotions will come from within the organization. Some serve the local community by providing hospital wards, recreational amenities and homes for the aged.

Non-economic objectives have growing importance in inter-national marketing and the philosophy of many multinational companies can be recognized within the above comments as can the importance of business ethics.

In international trade there are many opportunities for un-ethical, even illegal, practices. For example the raising of false invoices to reduce customs duties and the bribery of local officials. There can be no doubt that such practices are common among some international competitors. Nevertheless they should be avoided at all costs and business should be obtained by scrupulously fair means or not at all.

Packing Regulations

In chapter 3 brief reference was made to the existence of local restrictions and regulations in many markets determining packing materials and methods which are acceptable.

The problem must be researched carefully for every individual market, to ensure that any legislation on packing is understood and complied with.

It is of interest that despite the existence of a number of widely understood and accepted symbols indicating (for example 'keep dry', 'this side up', 'fragile', 'radioactive') there is no all embracing international agreement on these symbols for general freight. For air freight, however, there is an internationally accepted set of International Airlines Transport Association labels.

It is important that packages for export be clearly marked using waterproof and saltproof material on at least two sides. It will greatly simplify the task of freight forwarders, port authorities and customs officers if marks can be read easily, clearly identifying both the individual package and, most important, the destination. Any instructions should appear in both English and also the language of the country of destination.

For a number of markets the shipping marks must include weights. In the case of markets such as Switzerland and Colombia customs duties are based on gross weights.

Reference has already been made to directives issued by the European Commission. One directive that will affect every exporter to the European Community is a European Commission directive on packaging and packaging waste.

The objectives of this directive are:

- quantitative prevention of the production of packaging waste and qualitative improvement of any packaging waste;

- recovery of packaging waste produced;
- minimization of the final disposal of packaging waste.

The European Community has also established requirements for the classification, packaging and labelling of dangerous substances within the European Community.

The initial directive defined the hazards as toxic, corrosive or harmful and provided a list of substances classified according to the defined hazards. It also established the required symbols for indicating the particular hazards, and gave a series of risk and safety phrases in five European languages.

Requirements specified in the initial directive have now been implemented in the laws of the various member states of the European Community, for example, the classification, packaging and labelling regulations (CPL) in the United Kingdom and Gefahrstoff Verordnung in Germany.

The regulations operating in different markets concerning marking and labelling of goods vary widely. Although not a universal requirement, some countries insist that all imported goods which can be marked must be marked with the name of the country of origin. An example of this requirement is in the United States of America. Under the United States Tariff Act, all imported articles must be marked in a conspicuous place with the name of the country of origin in English, in such a manner that the marking will remain on the article until it reaches the final consumer.

Marks of origin must be shown on imported goods in general in Argentina, Cuba, Uruguay and the Philippines. In Chile all goods ordinarily consumed by the public must be marked to show the country of origin. Mexico requires an indication of origin for goods bearing trademarks registered in Mexico, if the exporter wants full protection under the Mexican trademark laws.

Many countries have extensive lists of products on which the country of origin must be marked, for example Australia, Denmark, France and Norway.

In India, Pakistan and Sri Lanka goods bearing descriptions in English but not produced in the United Kingdom are considered to be falsely described unless they bear a clear indication of the country of origin. In a similar way, goods exported to Brazil bearing labels in Portuguese, but not being products of Portugal must show the true country of origin.

In addition to declaring the country of origin, many countries have detailed regulations for the labelling of products such as foodstuffs, beverages, pharmaceutical and toilet preparations. Labels may have to show not only the name and address of the manufacturer, but also such items as a list of ingredients, weight or volume of contents and other relevant information. In many cases these descriptions must be in the language and weights and measures system of the importing country. Any trade description attached to a product must, of course, be accurate.

The use of national symbols, such as coats of arms and flags, is frequently restricted and the use of the Red Cross name or symbol is prohibited by international convention.

Import Duties and Quotas

In the early nineteen eighties the world economy was showing signs of growth in certain trades, while shipments of oil tended to remain static or decline. All such events are allied to economic factors, a major one being the availability of credit and the levels of interest rates especially for capital goods. As a result of violent changes in interest rates and other fiscal and economic measures, especially the growth in policies of nationalism, marketing opportunities can change very quickly, sometimes with disastrous results for the exporter. It is essential for countries to keep a close check on their balance of payments position and institute a number of checks and balances by way of import duties. Import duties serve two purposes. First and foremost they raise revenue, and they also serve to protect national manufacturers against competition from imported products.

In addition to import duties further problems may be created for an exporter by the imposition of quotas in the target markets overseas. Quotas may be imposed by a country in order to effect strict control over the volume of imported goods. Usually quotas will be based on the volume of imports from each country in a given year.

Mention has already been made of the importance of keeping delivery promises. Not only is this essential in order to establish and maintain good relations with your overseas customers, but becomes even more important where an order has been placed against a limited quota available to the importer.

Import Licences

Closely allied to the imposition of quotas in a market is the existence of import licensing restrictions. In order to regulate imports, some countries will, from time to time, impose import regulations in place of, or in addition to, tariffs. This provides a more precise method of control so that imports can be limited to certain predetermined amounts or indeed prohibited altogether.

Such restrictions may be imposed for either political or economic reasons. For example a country may operate an import licensing scheme either due to a shortage of foreign currency or possibly to restrict the inflow of imported goods in order to protect domestic industries. As a result of the growth of economic nationalism, home based industries are frequently favoured to the detriment of overseas exporters.

In some instances a country will impose an import licensing programme in conjunction with an exchange control scheme. In such an instance the restriction will apply not specifically to the imported goods themselves, but to obtaining exchange to pay for them which will of course result in a restriction on imports.

With such a scheme a country may resolve to classify imports and provide funds at officially set rates of exchange for each category. The more favourable treatment will be accorded to those goods which are considered to be essential to the economy of the country.

The General Agreement on Tariffs and Trade, GATT, prohibits in principle the use of quantitative restrictions on imports. However, it is accepted that this may not be possible in every country and certain clearly defined exceptions are permitted. One of the exceptions is that products of a kind which are controlled internally such as agricultural and fisheries products may be subject to import control. However, any such restrictions must be nondiscriminatory, that is to say, they must apply equally to all countries. It is, however, permitted by GATT to impose temporary restrictions for balance of payment reasons. As an exception, in such cases discriminatory application of restriction between sources of supply may be used.

As the balance of payments position improves in a country, this enables some import controls to be relaxed.

Trade with state controlled economies poses special problems. In these markets foreign trade is a monopoly of the state. Trade must be carried out exclusively with state corporations, each of which will deal with a particular category of goods, and buys and sells in accordance with the targets set by the country's short-term or long-term economic plans.

Wherever import licensing restrictions are in operation in a market the exporter must pay careful attention to two factors. Initially the exporter must ensure that the customer in the overseas market is able to obtain the appropriate import licence. Once this has been obtained he must discover the length of time for which the import licence is valid. In some cases, there may be a time limit imposed on the licence and in such a case it will be essential to ensure that delivery is made before the expiry date of the licence. Failure to deliver on time will not only deprive the exporter of the opportunity to sell his goods, but above all will result in a total loss of confidence by the overseas buyer which could well have a disastrous effect on future business prospects in the market.

It should be remembered that in addition to import restrictions imposed in certain overseas markets, certain products may be subject to export restrictions in the United Kingdom. The range of products which are subject to export licensing restrictions in the United Kingdom varies from what are considered to be strategic commodities to works of art or certain items of special historical interest. Strategic items include a range of high-tech products, armaments, materials and equipment concerned with the nuclear industries. In the case of strategic commodities, the export licensing controls may well apply to certain specified countries only.

If a company is proposing to export goods which are subject to an export licence, it will of course be essential to take the necessary steps to obtain the appropriate export licence before processing the corresponding order.

Product Modification

Because a product has sold successfully in the home market, and possibly in certain overseas markets, it will not necessarily follow that it will be acceptable on a worldwide basis. Indeed, when proposing to enter an overseas market, it is important to undertake detailed research to establish if it may be necessary to modify the product in any way to ensure acceptability to an overseas market.

Perhaps one of the most obvious areas where modification will be essential is the case of electrical goods. The problem most frequently encountered will be the differing voltages and frequencies in use in a market. These must be researched together with the need to comply with any safety or quality standards which may have to be met. Unless these potential problems are researched and overcome, it will, quite simply, be impossible to sell your products in a market.

Examples of products which will require varying degrees of modification to ensure acceptance in a market are motor vehicles. In addition to the question of right hand or left hand drive, some markets as for example the United States of America and Japan impose very strict rules and regulations on exhaust emissions. In addition, headlamps will also require certain modification in order to meet the regulations in force in a number of markets.

An important essential before entering a market is to undertake a detailed study of tastes and fashions prevailing in the market. When considering these it would be easy to think only in terms of items such as clothing, an obvious example of an area where these factors are of paramount importance. However, there is an extensive range of consumer goods where tastes will vary in each market and fashions will be changing from year to year. Unless these factors are researched and considered, it would be very easy to find that your product, whatever its success in other markets, may be considered old-fashioned and out of date. Similarly, before considering the introduction of any new design features in a product, it must be confirmed that these will be acceptable in the target market.

There may well be instances where your product is facing serious competition in a market, either from domestic products or from other imported items. In such an instance, the secret of success may lie in modifying your product in order to increase its competitiveness.

Another factor which can call for product modification is a situation in which a product may be nearing the end of its life cycle. However, product modification may well be the means of prolonging the life cycle and possibly modifying the product to make it acceptable in a new market.

For a number of items, an important factor to be considered will be colour. In some overseas markets colours which would be totally acceptable in the home market may have totally different meanings. For example, in the home market white is normally associated with purity, cleanliness and weddings; in South East Asian markets it is the colour which is associated with death and mourning.

Yet another factor which must be considered very carefully is pack size. An example of the importance of this factor can be seen in the normal pack sizes which are commonly used in North America for products such as washing powders and cereals. These are usually very much larger than the sizes which would normally be encountered in the home market. This is, of course, a further example of the way in which tastes vary in different markets. In the case of this example part of the answer lies in different shopping habits. In North America, customers are likely to make less frequent visits to supermarkets, hypermarkets and out of town stores to make purchases in bulk. At the other end of the scale, some retail outlets in certain African countries will sell very small quantities, even single items, for such products as razor blades, which in other markets would not be sold in this manner. The growth of supermarkets in the United Kingdom has over recent years shown a significant change in pack size for a number of products.

Careful consideration must be given to the labelling of products. There are two aspects which must be investigated.

First and foremost it is essential to investigate the rules and regulations which apply to labelling in a market. These vary from market to market and involve specific requirements as to what information must legally appear on a label, also the possible requirement to produce labels in the language of the country in question. The second important aspect of labelling is to consider how this may be used as a marketing tool. There are many labels which are instantly recognizable and this obviously helps to ensure that consumers choose your products. Examples are Heinz and their well known '57' symbol and the readily recognizable packaging used by Kodak products. Another brand name which has become recognized on a worldwide basis is Coca Cola with its distinctive type style.

Products may frequently be modified by, for example, the use of alternative materials possibly yielding different levels of performance.

A very common reason for product modification is in order to improve the quality and consequently the acceptability of a product. It is possible that an effort to build up extra quality as perceived by an engineer, through the use of higher grade materials, may not necessarily have the desired effect of increasing quality as perceived by the customer. There are four levels of quality improvement in descending order of impact on the market:

1 improvement that is readily recognized as such by the majority of buyers, affecting both the appearance of the product, and also its performance;
2 improvement that is not at once visually observable by the buyers, but will become apparent in improved product performance once the customers have tried it;
3 improvement in quality that is aimed at a specialized end-user, and only significant for a proportion of the customers;
4 improvement in the product that not only cannot be perceived visually but cannot be detected in the product function. The existence of such an improvement must be taken on trust by the buyer. An example of such a product is a proprietary medicine.

In seeking constantly to improve product performance, a company may modify its product quality in each of the four ways at the same time. This explains why some modified products gain acceptance more easily in the market place.

Frequently it may be resolved to improve features of a product in order to increase the number of real or imagined product benefits. An example of such a modification would be modern cameras. Early cameras were bulky, heavy and had limited capabilities. With improvements in materials, lenses and shutters, a series of alternative speeds became available, and miniature versions were developed. Further product modification led to the introduction of such features as built-in range finders, built-in exposure meters and flash connections. Such feature improvements are intended to increase the range and scale of the products used. They can, of course, be adapted to appeal to special sections of the market. The introduction of the instant camera, producing prints at the time of exposure may be seen in this light.

Modifications may be made to improve the aesthetic appeal of a product, rather than its functional performance. In the case of certain products, superior styling could even outweigh some functional disadvantages. When considering style improvements the three most common variables are colour, shape and texture. In repeat purchase markets style improvement may be limited to packaging or pack design. Most buyers will respond favourably to good clear presentation. An important factor to remember is that style and fashion will vary from one market to another and will also be influenced by climatic conditions.

In certain instances, it may be decided to change the formulation of a product in order to improve performance, or at least maintain a constant level of performance while reducing costs. In such a case the intrinsic value of each component part of a product and the function which it has to perform is questioned and analysed. The replacement of certain materials by a lower grade or cheaper alternative, providing that it does not affect the performance of the product in relation to the customer's expectations, may have a dramatic effect on the competitiveness of the product.

This type of value analysis technique has been developed

over a number of years as a means of maintaining or even increasing company profit margins.

As a result of increased competition and diminishing profit margins a manufacturer may resolve to reduce the quality of a product in order either to cheapen it, or to maintain its profitability.

Great thought should be given to such a proposal, as product durability and performance have a significant influence on buyers' choices in overseas markets. Nevertheless, there are numerous examples of products which are in fact over-engineered and which therefore present opportunities to effect reductions in production costs whilst still maintaining an acceptable quality.

In some instances, an alternative to quality reduction is quantity reduction. This is particularly applicable in the case, for example, of packaged foods and confectionery. By making small reductions in quantities over a period of time, while still maintaining quality, it may well be possible to reduce costs and still retain customers who might well have been lost had the quality of the product been down-graded. For the smaller company in competition with larger organizations, it may be possible to increase competitiveness by initiating service improvements.

In addition to the various forms of product modification previously referred to, some companies may seek to improve their position in the market by introducing a variety of promotional benefits.

Methods of adding value to a product by means of promotional benefits range from competitions, give-aways, premiums or holidays, any of which will serve as short-term inducements to buy.

Non-tariff Barriers

In chapter 8 reference was made to import licences and quotas, both of which are non-tariff barriers to trade.

Due very largely to growing policies of national independence in some markets, an ever growing problem facing exporters is a tendency for markets to introduce a growing range of non-tariff barriers. These restrictions will frequently take the form of special technical or safety standards, restrictions on the contents of foodstuffs, or special labelling requirements. In addition, countries may impose special requirements in connection with the information which must appear on invoices.

These non-tariff barriers are imposed to protect home based industries, many of which, in an early stage of development, would find it difficult to compete effectively with imported goods which would not only be available at competitive prices, but would frequently be of superior design, finish and quality and would therefore be more attractive to the end user.

Markets in which non-tariff barriers are ever more common are state controlled economies where foreign trade is a state monopoly.

Where non-tariff barriers exist, it may be impossible to undertake direct exports and consideration must be given to alternative methods of penetration.

Reference has already been made to the sale of knowhow, which in a variety of forms provides an excellent way to penetrate a market which might otherwise be closed due to a variety of non-tariff barriers. In addition to the options already mentioned, there are growing opportunities to consider what is known as a turnkey operation. Many countries with barriers to direct imports will welcome a venture whereby the target market will encourage overseas manufacturers to invest both finance, equipment and expertise. Such an arrangement provides the exporter with an opportunity to penetrate a market which would otherwise be closed and enables the host country to improve its own production capabilities.

In a turnkey operation, the exporter will provide the necessary equipment and expertise and construct a plant in an overseas market. Not only will the exporter construct and operate the plant but will also provide the necessary expert staff, first of all to commission the plant, but also to train local staff before eventually turning the operation over to the overseas customer.

Industrial cooperation agreements, franchising, management contracts and contract manufacture are also further ways in which it may be possible to penetrate a market which would otherwise be closed to normal export trade.

Questions for Discussion

1 Identify the uncontrollable variables which must be considered in overseas markets.

2 Discuss various problems to be considered in order to meet overseas restrictions and regulations determining acceptable packing materials and methods.

3 What do you understand by the term 'non-tariff barrier'?

9

The Needs of
Regulatory Bodies

National Standards

Careful consideration must be given to a wide range of legislation and legal constraints which may be encountered in overseas markets.

It can be argued that in any country 'Marketing is Marketing' and any special legal, technical or economic factors which apply in a particular market are in fact part of the overall marketing problems which must be overcome anywhere. In this sense marketing overseas is no different from marketing in the United Kingdom once one accepts that in an overseas market it will be necessary to identify and resolve a greater range of problems. Initially it is important to be aware of the areas in which restrictions to trade may be encountered in a market overseas. These restrictions apply very frequently in areas such as foodstuff additives, labelling and packaging requirements and also permitted advertising copy. These restrictions may apply in individual markets or in wider trading blocs.

In addition to the above, many countries have their own safety regulations which must be met. These will frequently apply to items such as electrical goods and mechanical equipment. The restrictions and their application will vary in each market. In some Scandinavian markets for example, it is not permitted to import electrical equipment until this has been submitted to the appropriate national standards authority for testing and has been granted official approval. Similarly a wide variety of technical and safety standards must be met before many countries will accept imported motor vehicles. Such regulations are very important in markets such as the United States and Japan. An important factor to remember is that these regulations are subject to continuous change and must therefore be kept under constant review.

An invaluable source of information and guidance on the various standards which must be met in an overseas market is Technical Help for Exporters (THE) a service operated by the British Standards Institution (BSI) under contract to the Department of Trade and Industry, to provide exporters with technical information on standards, laws, regulations and approval schemes. It is interesting to note that the BSI's library is the world's leading standards library having over five hundred thousand technical documents, supported by a large number of experts in a wide range of specialist areas.

THE provides exporters with an enquiry service. On contacting them they will answer questions on foreign regulations and standards and foreign certification and approval bodies.

At the time of writing, questions up to half an hour in duration are being answered free of charge. When a more detailed analysis of a foreign market is required this can be provided by a THE engineering consultant. Working with a potential exporter for up to three days, a consultant will help with the following:

- identify relevant regulations and governing bodies;
- create approval plans;
- discuss the application of standards to your products.

If a company employs less than two hundred people and has not previously made use of the engineering consultancy service, a discount is made on the normal consultancy fees.

The United States is an example of a market which has a wide range of standards which must first of all be identified and then complied with.

The United States electrical standards vary considerably from most British standards. Whereas in the United Kingdom, electrical standards are largely concerned with shock hazard, United States standards stress the elimination of fire risks. The names of American standards writing bodies, such as Factory Mutual, Underwriters Laboratories and National Fire Protection Association indicate their insurance based origins. The United Kingdom and the United States have different voltages and frequencies. In addition the general field of electrical engineering in the United Kingdom uses the metric system to a much greater extent than is the case in the United States or Canada.

Attempts are being made to establish some harmonization of standards through the International Electrotechnical Commission (IEC), however, it is likely that major differences will continue for some time.

In the United States, there are well over four hundred bodies producing standards, in addition to government bodies producing technical regulations which affect the design and manufacture of goods sold throughout the United States. The American National Standards Institute (ANSI) normally republishes standards produced by other bodies.

When considering exporting to the United States, it is also necessary to consider the Federal Government Departments which issue technical regulations. Examples of these regulations include the rules on computing devices issued by the Federal Communications Commission (FCC), rules on Visual Display Unit screens issued by the Bureau of Radiological Health and the controls which apply to electro-medical devices, published by the Food and Drug Administration (FDA).

Details of the United States standards regulations and approval procedures are available from the British Standards Institution.

It is simpler to identify which standard a product must meet in Canada as electrical standards are written by a single body: the Canadian Standards Association (CSA).

The creation of the single European market in 1993 was designed among other things to make it easier for exporters of goods and services to carry out their business within the European Community. In order to achieve this end, barriers between countries in the European Community arising from differences in technical standards are being dismantled by harmonizing different national standards.

In May 1985 the European Council of Ministers decided on a change of procedures that became known as the New Approach to Technical Harmonization and Standards. Directives produced post 1985 are generally referred to as new approach directives.

The process of harmonization begins with the issue of directives which are documents issued by the European Commission as statements of intent and goals to be achieved in a specific area such as, for example, personal protective equipment or electromagnetic compatibility. These directives are eventually turned into reality by the production of standards by the European Committees for Standardization (CEN, CENELEC).

The first directives to be produced, and which must be complied with before goods can be sold anywhere in the European Community, cover the following:

- simple pressure vessels;
- safety of toys;
- construction products;
- electromagnetic compatibility;
- machinery safety;
- personal protective equipment;
- non-automatic weighing machines;
- active implantable medical devices;
- appliances burning gaseous fuels;
- telecommunications terminal equipment;
- medical devices.

For many products a relevant European Standard harmonized for use across the Community will already exist. In the United Kingdom, harmonized standards are designated BS or EN followed by a number. A comprehensive list of standards relevant to a particular product can be identified from the BSI catalogue.

Products conforming with the requirements of directives are then able to bear the CE mark, which should mean that they can be sold within the Community.

In some instances, a product may be required to comply with more than one directive. For example, industrial machinery may have to comply with both the machinery safety and also the electromagnetic compatibility directives.

As will be appreciated from the foregoing the range of barriers to trade created by differing legislation and standards which have to be met is very extensive. It is of paramount importance that exporters investigate and understand these requirements before attempting to market their goods overseas.

Technical Help for Exporters will provide invaluable assistance and guidance on potential problems. In so far as the European Community is concerned, THE suggests that a potential exporter should answer the following questions:

1 Does the product fall within the scope of a technical or new approach directive?

2 If 'yes' do you know which standards you will use to demonstrate that the product meets the essential requirements?

3 (a) Are you required to use the CE mark?
   (b) Do you understand the CE mark regulations?

4 Will testing or certification by a third party be required in your product area?

5 Are you fully aware of the potential impact of current or future packaging and labelling directives?

6 In addition to harmonized standards are you aware of the local regulatory requirements in your key markets within Europe?

7 If harmonized standards do not exist, are you aware of the current state of development in your field?

8 Do you have the mechanism continually to monitor changes and developments in standards or regulations?

9 Is the impact of harmonized standards being fully integrated into the new product development process?

10 Are you looking at the potential benefits of product or part rationalization through the adoption of European standards?

11 Will directives in non-product areas such as health and safety in the work place affect your operations?

12 Have you considered the impact of BS5750/EN29000 on your European operations and overall business efficiency? (BS5750 and EN29000, unlike most other standards, do not apply to specific products. They are internationally accepted standards which apply to quality systems, quality control

and other aspects. In other words, confirmation of an organization's ability to undertake specified tasks and processes.
As an internationally accepted standard they replace, for
example, lists of manufacturers who in the past were
approved by the Department of Trade and Industry to
undertake government contracts.)

13 Will the directive covering public procurement have an
impact on your major customer purchasing activities?

14 Do you know in which countries outside Europe your
product will be accepted because of its compliance with
European standards?

If the exporter is uncertain about any of the answers, the next
step must be to discuss them with THE who will be in a
position to provide invaluable advice. BSI publishes a Quarterly
Newsletter which is essential reading for exporters. The
publication is *INSTEP*, short for *International News on
Standards and Exporting*. It is aimed to keep exporters up to
date with changing information needs on standards and
technical requirements worldwide.

Marketing Knowhow

In chapter 6, considering various methods of selling, reference
was made to the growing market for the sale of knowhow.

It must be stressed that this relatively new marketing opportunity has arisen due to a wide variety of legal restrictions
which may be imposed in a market to restrict imports.

Reference has been made to some of the restrictions which
may be imposed in a market, either to conserve foreign currency
or protect local industries.

Non-tariff barriers are frequently imposed when a country has
a developing economy and is anxious not only to establish but
also to protect and increase its own domestic industries.

In an overseas marketing environment, local competition is
an influential factor. It may be possible to consider various
approaches. For example, to consider if it may be possible to
enter a market with an amended or cheaper version of one's

own standard product. Alternatively, it may be possible to trade up beyond the abilities of the local manufacturers to exploit a relatively affluent and unexplored segment of the market. In either case any decision will be based on the results of a market research exercise.

In some western-style economies, local competition is well entrenched and successful. As a result it will be difficult, if not impossible, to export successfully to such markets. In such cases it would be important for the imported product to go one better in either price, quality, design, durability or other factors. There would obviously be no hope for a potential exporter who was deficient in the basics of reliability, quality, price, commercial efficiency, speed of delivery and, where appropriate, effective after-sales service.

Considering the potential problems will underline the possible benefits of considering the sale of knowhow. Not only will such an approach overcome a variety of both tariff or non-tariff barriers to trade, it will also present the possibility of a profitable venture with an established domestic producer.

In many instances such an arrangement may present the only possibility of doing business in a given market.

Licensing

It frequently happens that it is virtually impossible to develop direct exports to a market due to a variety of import barriers, such as high landed costs, non-tariff barriers or an inability to compete with other exporters. If you are confronted with these problems it may be wise to consider if you have a patent, a special product, process or even a trademark which is of value.

Should this be the case, the possible solution may well be to consider the export of knowhow by entering into a licensing agreement with an overseas manufacturer. Licensing could well provide an entrée to a new and potentially profitable export opportunity.

An obvious advantage of entering into a licensing agreement with a manufacturer overseas is that it may well be the only possible means of doing business in a market, by selling to overseas manufacturers the right to use blueprints, specifications, manufacturing processes and technical assistance for products or processes.

Developing countries seek possibilities to develop their industrialization to attain economic growth, and frequently impose barriers to protect infant domestic industries.

These needs in developing countries offer opportunities to owners of manufacturing processes and patents who have never previously engaged in exporting. Although mention was made of developing countries, there are many instances when countries with well developed economies will welcome an opportunity to acquire new techniques and expertise.

An essential preliminary consideration is the need to undertake detailed market research to establish the potential market for your product or process and also to explore fully the position of a potential licensee in his own home market.

An important aim will be to discover a licensee who is well established in the market and who will probably already be producing similar or complementary products which are being sold to an established clientele.

Why should an established manufacturer overseas be interested in obtaining a licence to produce your goods? In many cases the attraction will be an opportunity to upgrade existing products or to introduce an additional complementary product.

Consideration should be given to the potential benefits which an exporter may receive from entering into a licensing agreement. This would include, for example:

- knowhow fee;
- service fees;
- royalties;
- technical improvement;
- exports of components or raw materials.

A fee is usually charged for the disclosure of all available technical data and also for access to any future research and development for the licensed product or process. An initial payment is made on signing the licensing agreement and this must cover the cost of transferring the required technical data.

If no specific patents are involved, the initial fee should be as high as possible, even if this means agreeing to lower service and royalty fees.

The service fee will be calculated either as a percentage of sales or as a specific amount per unit or per period of time. The service fee is levied to finance continued technical assistance, and is applied to the balance outstanding on the agreed knowhow fee. After the agreed knowhow fee has been discharged, there will frequently be agreement on a reduction of the service fee.

Royalties will become payable on the agreed use of the licensor's trademark and are generally calculated in the same manner as the service fee, but without any later reduction in the rate.

It is wise to keep service and royalty fees separate as certain countries levy little or no tax on service fees but may well apply maximum rates to royalties. In some instances, a country may resolve to apply limits to the royalties which may be paid.

There is always a possibility that after having received technical assistance from the exporter, a licensee may develop improved products or production methods. Agreement will frequently specify that the licensor may have access to and make use of any such improvement.

With some licensing agreements, at least in the initial stages, provision may be made for the licensor to supply certain components or raw materials. This will produce an additional source of profit for the licensor.

Conclusion of a satisfactory licensing agreement is often a lengthy and involved process because both parties are anxious to be fully protected. The licensing agreement should reflect the thoughts and intentions of both parties, the result being a satisfactory agreement based upon good faith. In some instances, an agreement must be approved by an overseas government, and in any case, competent legal advice should be sought before finalizing the agreement.

Listed overleaf are a number of elements which must be considered when entering into a licensing agreement with a company overseas:

1 A clear definition of the products, processes or trademarks to be licensed.
2 Country or clearly defined area in which the licensee will have rights to manufacture and sell.
3 Is the licensee to have the right to sell only in the agreed area, or a larger area? The licensor should retain the right to change the area if conditions make this necessary. For example, if sales in the area originally agreed do not meet original targets.
4 If the agreement involves the use of the licensor's trademark, it is important to establish whether this alone is to be applied to the product, or if it is to be used in combination with the licensee's trademark. Many cases occur where the use of a combination trademark will be desirable. However, should this be the chosen option, there should be a condition in the agreement that the joint trademark be discontinued should the agreement be terminated.
5 It is important to determine who shall be responsible to defend any trademark infringement. Normally this will be undertaken by the licensor with cooperation and assistance from the licensee.
6 From the outset, it is important to define production and sales targets, with the licensor retaining the right to terminate the agreement or be compensated should these targets not be met.
7 Agreement must be reached and set out in the formal document, as to whether the licensee will be allowed to produce similar or competitive products.
8 What technical assistance will be provided by the licensor?
9 The licensee will probably wish to send employees for training by the licensor, and seek visits by technical staff from the licensor. The maximum number of such visits should be specified, together with agreement on who will meet the cost.
10 It is important to ensure that products will be manufactured in accordance with agreed specifications and standards of quality. Arrangements should be made to ensure that a facility is made available to inspect the licensee's operation, also to be able to monitor articles manufactured by the licensee.

11 The licensor should be prepared to be flexible about possible changes to design, while retaining the right to approve any proposed changes.

12 It will be necessary to agree who will own the technical information when the agreement terminates.

13 It is possible that a licensee may develop from the original technical assistance certain improvements or new production methods. Hopefully, it will be possible to agree on a reverse flow of information.

14 Agreement should be reached on the provision of regular product and sales reports, together with a right of audit.

15 The duration of the agreement must be clearly defined together with arrangements both for termination and possible renewal.

Usually agreements will be for a period of five or ten years, depending on the time taken to commence production, and the initial investment by the licensee.

16 It will be necessary to specify whether the licensee will have the right to assign or sub-licence to a third party. In most cases, this would only be allowed with specific approval by the licensor.

17 Obviously the object of the agreement is to enable the exporter to enter a market and derive profits from the agreement. A possible problem which must be considered is the licensee's ability to pay, bearing in mind the possibility of difficulties being created by exchange regulations. In some cases the licensee may have a foreign account outside his own country, from which he would be able to guarantee payment. In some markets government approval of a licensing agreement will carry with it the automatic right to obtain foreign exchange. An important aspect to be investigated will be the tax position in the overseas market. It must be clearly established if fees may be subject to any local tax.

18 Any agreement, to be a success, must be based on good faith. Consideration must therefore be given to what action will follow should the licensee decide to sell out.

19 In cases where agreement has been reached for the licensee to import materials or components, it must be established what restrictions, if any, may be applied to their use.

20 A further important undertaking to be obtained from licensees is that they will comply with all the necessary laws and regulations in operation in the market.

21 The agreement will normally provide for automatic termination in the event of bankruptcy of the licensee.

22 The agreement should also specify arrangements for undertaking any appropriate advertising and sales promotion.

The foregoing list contains some of the basic elements which should be taken into consideration when entering into a licensing agreement. The laws and regulations governing licensing agreements will vary in each country, and appropriate research must be undertaken in each potential market.

Licensing agreements can be beneficial both for the licensor and the licensee. This point is well illustrated by cases where manufacturing licences have been granted to an overseas manufacturer and have continued in operation even after the licensor has discontinued production of the product. An example of this is the Volkswagen Beetle, which continued to be manufactured in Brazil after the original production in Germany had been discontinued. Similarly when production of the Mini Moke was discontinued in the United Kingdom, production still continued in Portugal.

Just as United Kingdom manufacturers will enter into agreements with overseas companies to produce their products under licence, there are numerous examples of overseas companies who have entered into agreements with British companies to produce their products under licence in the United Kingdom as, for example, Carlsberg and Fosters beers.

An interesting example of how to research and then exploit overseas markets is the philosophy adopted by Guinness Exports to investigate markets and establish an extensive range of new outlets overseas.

Initially, the company undertook extensive research in a number of overseas markets. This research covered not only the existing local production and availability of beers, but also paid special attention to tastes which would be acceptable. It is interesting to appreciate that, wherever it is sold, the product and packaging are instantly recognizable. However, a great deal of attention is given to provide a taste which is totally acceptable in a market and which will involve a modest adjustment to the original flavour. Although the labels will be instantly recognizable, they contain minor modifications to meet the specific needs of each individual market.

Where the company's market research and test marketing indicated promising opportunities, trade was commenced by exporting Guinness brewed in the United Kingdom. In each market a specific sales target was set and when this was reached, the company entered into a licensing agreement with an overseas brewer to produce and market Guinness under licence.

Franchising

In chapter 6, reference was made to franchising when considering various types of sales organization. As a result of the variety of political and legal constraints which have to be overcome in certain markets, in addition to possible non-tariff barriers, franchising may well present a means of entering a market where other methods of trade would not be possible. Whereas agreement could be reached for manufacturers to produce patented goods overseas under licence, franchising would be the available option for products or services which cannot be patented.

Very frequently a franchising operation will involve the use of and exploitation of a trademark. Some very sound advice on the choice of a trademark name was given by George Eastman, the originator of Kodak, a trademark which is readily recognized throughout the world. His advice was to choose a trade name which is short, vigorous, incapable of being misspelled, and in order to satisfy trademark laws, it should mean absolutely nothing. Choice of a word which could have a totally different meaning in certain countries could well lead to a variety of problems. An example of the creation of a successful and widely recognized brand name is PG Tips, a product of Brooke Bond, the world's largest tea company.

In 1932, Brooke Bond launched Digestive Tea, as at that time tea was promoted for its medicinal properties. Indeed some brands were stocked by chemists. In 1945 the Ministry of Health called a halt to health claims for tea and a new name had to be found. The chosen name was Pre-Gestee, an evocation of the digestive theme but labelled with the declaration 'Brooke Bond do not claim any medicinal, nutritional or dietary value for their tea'.

Quarter pound packets were marketed and were marked PG, an abbreviation of the new name by which customers soon came to identify the brand. By 1951 Brooke Bond had adopted the initials officially and added the Tips in reference to the blend's exclusive use of the most succulent tips from the leaves of the tea plant. Eventually, in 1955, PG Tips was registered as a brand name.

Although only introduced in 1970 in the United Kingdom, tea bags now account for seventy per cent of PG Tips sales, which amount to the equivalent of sixty million cups per day.

There are certain precautions which must be undertaken when entering into a franchising agreement. Initially it is important that the franchisor makes a thorough investigation of the prospective franchisee's operation to ensure that it will be possible to maintain the standards set by the franchisor. In the event of agreement being reached, the franchisor will initiate procedures to enable a constant check to be kept on the operation of the franchisee. Depending on the type of business for which a franchise is granted the franchisor will provide all the necessary technical back up, materials, where appropriate, and, most importantly, staff training.

Once a franchise agreement has been reached, it will be imperative that the franchisee preserves the standards and image already created by the franchisor. Of growing importance for the granting of franchises are fast food outlets, all of which must ensure that they maintain the image and standards created by the franchisor.

Questions for Discussion

1 Where would you obtain information on international standards?

2 Give three examples of marketing 'knowhow'.

3 Describe the major differences between licensing and franchising.

10

United Kingdom Marketing and Exporting: Similarities and Differences

Marketing in the United Kingdom does not present major problems, such as one might expect to encounter in overseas markets. First and foremost the market is readily accessible, the methods of trading are familiar, as are the potential outlets and channels of distribution.

Similarly, there are no major barriers to trade or unfamiliar rules and regulations which must be complied with. In addition trade is greatly facilitated by the absence of any language problems.

However, all the above mentioned factors may well cause problems when exporting. An effort will now be made to underline the similarities and differences between United Kingdom marketing and exporting.

Similarities

Marketing strategy

A marketing strategy based on user-orientation and an adequate return on investment would seem to be a satisfactory approach to all markets, either home or overseas. It is true to say that for advanced industrial countries, a marketing plan will look much the same from one country to another. In all probability the product will have to be designed to the same broad technical standards. The patterns of distribution will be similar, in many cases the available promotional media will be the same. It may well be that a certain degree of standardization of products will be the outcome of the widespread use of advertising. A number of companies have designed and sold their products in Europe, helped to some degree by the creation of the European Economic Community, and inevitably this has helped to produce a degree of uniformity in technical, commercial and legal matters. Research has been undertaken to determine if it might be possible to standardize the advertising message for the European Community, admitting of no subjective or psychological differences, but requiring merely an appropriate translation from country to country. On the other hand the marketing plans for third world countries may look very different, taking into consideration the fact that they have important user factors, deriving from significant cultural and religious differences, rudimentary systems of distribution and sales promotion, and in certain instances levels of literacy that permit no more than pictorial treatment for an advertising message.

A further area to be considered is the market selection decision. This will involve a range of alternative strategies. These must be realistically conditioned by the resources available so as to achieve a planned and profit-maximizing market operation. Once again it is important to undertake adequate research into the potential of each market.

Market selection

When selecting a market, either in the United Kingdom or overseas, various important factors must be considered. The major matters to be researched are detailed below and it will be appreciated that these factors must be taken into consideration in all markets:

- present and potential size of market;
- degree and type of competition;
- prevailing price levels;

- necessary degree of advertising and promotional activities;
- comparisons with competition;
- any barriers to trade;
- fixing of sales targets;
- estimation of projected profits.

In the case of the home market, it will be necessary to seek advice from a number of sources, such as banks, chambers of commerce, trade associations and the Confederation of British Industry.

For overseas markets it will be necessary to supplement the above mentioned sources of information by including, for example:

- the Department of Trade and Industry;
- the British Standards Institution;
- United Kingdom embassies in foreign countries;
- the Institute of Export;
- the Institute of Freight Forwarders.

As will be appreciated from the foregoing, market selection (wherever the market) will involve seeking information from a wide range of sources and undertaking detailed research to determine the prospects and potential in each market.

Decision making

An essential prerequisite to enable marketing decisions to be made, is to undertake a market research programme. This must be the first step for either the home market or markets overseas. In both cases it is important to remember that market research cannot be regarded as a one-off operation but must be a continuous function in any marketing programme.

A successful marketing programme – whether at home or overseas – depends heavily on the systematic investigation, recording, analysis and presentation of facts and figures concerning the contractual and physical movement of goods and services between supplier and consumer. Irrespective of the market being researched, marketing research will involve the following activities.

1 Consumer research which is concerned with customers' attitudes, actions, preferences and reactions in respect of a particular marketing situation.
2 Market research which considers the location, present and future potential of markets, encompassing such areas of study as the patterns of trade, channels of distribution and activities of competitors.
3 Advertising research, which concerns the attempt to evaluate the impact and effectiveness of advertising by means of a study of consumers' reactions to advertising programmes.
4 Test marketing which is frequently used as a sequel to either consumer or market research in order to substantiate the viability of a marketing plan.

In any market it is marketing research that provides the basis on which marketing decisions can be made.

It is often said that the findings of good marketing research are invaluable. Investigations may indicate that a certain course of action is worth pursuing or they might suggest that little or no success will be achieved in a particular field.

Such indications are most important as they will enable management to reach decisions either to pursue certain lines of action, or to discard as unviable some preconceived plan. As a result of a market research operation, for example, it might be resolved to increase production capacity; this could involve substantial capital outlay on plant and machinery as well as additional storage and other facilities; there might also be an increase in variable production costs through extra labour and overheads.

Whatever the market under consideration such decisions, once made, are difficult to reverse or turn to alternative advantage, especially where specific objectives are concerned, while much of the capital expenditure may be largely wasted or at best, will fall well below optimum effectiveness.

Market research will also provide indications on the appropriate sales force which will be required to achieve the planned objectives. In addition the information obtained will be an invaluable guide to enable the right decision to be made in order to devise a general marketing plan. Before such a plan is fully implemented it should be either validated or disproved by undertaking a test marketing.

It will be appreciated that whatever the market, a wide range of important decisions must be made to produce a successful marketing programme.

Sales personnel

Products simply do not sell themselves however well designed and competitively priced they may be. Selecting, training and supervising a sales force is of paramount importance for any company.

Sales personnel must first and foremost be selected with care, taking account of their potential capabilities, attitudes and possible previous experience with similar or complimentary products.

It is most important that all sales personnel should receive detailed training, covering the company, its business methods and objectives and above all comprehensive product and policy knowledge.

Having selected, trained and introduced new personnel to the sales force it is very important to devise and implement a procedure to control, supervise and provide the best possible back up for a sales force.

Whatever the market, it is important that members of the sales force should not only be good salespeople themselves but above all should be regarded as good ambassadors for the company. It also has to be remembered that in the eyes of a customer the salesman is looked upon as 'the company'. Chosen with care, trained, encouraged and supported, good members of a sales team may well spell the difference between success and failure.

Having made the statement that products simply do not sell themselves, it has to be said that there will always be exceptions to any rule. It must be stressed that in the field of overseas marketing, the prospect of having a product which is truly unique and has worldwide appeal is extremely rare. For this reason, detailed below is the history of one such very rare product, the cat's eye.

Percy Shaw, a Yorkshireman, had over the years invented a variety of products, none of which had any great success. It is said that one foggy night he was driving from Bradford to Halifax. Usually he had no difficulty in finding his way as he could see in his headlight beam tramlines which he could follow. On this particular night the tramlines had been taken up for repair and he was heading for a steep drop at the side of the road. At the last moment his headlights picked up two points of light. These were the eyes of a cat sitting on a fence post at the edge of the drop.

Percy Shaw survived, and from this experience the well-known cats' eyes were developed, in the form of self-cleaning reflectors sunk in the road surface.

Percy Shaw manufactured his first cats' eyes in 1934 since when, because of their unique attributes, countless millions have been sold to be used in virtually every country in the world. It is estimated that this single, unique product enabled him to make a fortune of some £11m.

Differences

Cultural and economic

Trading in overseas markets involves overcoming a wide range of cultural and economic barriers. On the cultural side it will readily be appreciated that the general European culture varies significantly from the cultures of (for examples) Africa, the Middle East and South East Asia. Many of these markets represent significant trading opportunities. Not only will there be the need to meet ever growing competition from worldwide sources, but above all to study and understand the different cultures, customs, habits, preferences and religious beliefs which are very different from those in the home market; it is essential to make a detailed study of these factors before preparing a marketing plan which will have any prospect of being successful.

Another vital area to be investigated is the economic position and also the political stability of overseas markets. Regarding the economic position, it is readily apparent that trading conditions in a state controlled economy will present special problems. It is also important to be aware of the varying levels of economic development in certain overseas markets.

The decision to trade in overseas markets will impose special problems for a company and will call for special capabilities and inclinations in the export marketing staff. It will be important for senior staff to travel extensively, to negotiate at policy level, often in a foreign language and above all to undertake an important and ongoing research function, all in addition to their normal selling duties.

Languages

Competence in foreign languages is an invaluable asset when marketing overseas. Reference has already been made to the importance of correct translation of material for advertising and general promotion and publicity material. The importance of perfect translation is well illustrated by the following extracts from a well-known Japanese trade journal. The journal itself is well produced and written in excellent English with the exception of one advertisement by a manufacturer of baking ovens, from which the following is taken:

The excellent performance of our ovens is authenticated by the mechanisms as mentioned below.
Strong powered circulation fan makes heat to go round the baking chamber without loss so that heat keeps itself to the minimum from going out of the stack and thereby the consumption of fuel is reduced to the least. Forcible convertion fan for hot air inside the ovens increases the thermal efficiency so greatly that assurance is given to the production of tasteful bread resultant from the evenness and full penetration of heat into its inhermost part, auto-matic thermal control equipment invariably keeps the baking chamber at a given temperature. Air curtain fixed to

the doorway prevents the oven's heat from escaping in case of the pans going in and out. Besides above, other various structure, such as automatic discharging device etc., makes the baking efficiency much more and also strikingly conduce to more diminution of the operatives around the oven.

Although it is quite easy to understand what the message is intended to convey, the presentation is totally unacceptable. The above example illustrates the disastrous results which can follow from attempting a literal translation of material from one language to another.

A further example of inappropriate translation occurred in October 1969 when a successful British Week was launched in Vienna. This promotion received whole hearted support from the local retailers, one of whom provided an excellent example of the inexplicable translations which sometimes appear. A menswear boutique, obviously anxious to give full support to the British Week proclaimed itself 'White Horse Tavern and Family Hotel'.

These notes emphasize the vital importance of being truly fluent in a language before making any attempt to conduct business negotiations. It would be wrong to think that a knowledge of a language which may well be perfectly adequate to cope with situations which may be encountered on an overseas holiday would be of any use in a business situation.

In order to be successful in an overseas marketing operation, not only is total fluency in a language essential, but it is also vital to be able to handle commercial and technical terminology.

Legal issues

Great care must be taken to study very carefully the different legal requirements which must be complied with in overseas markets.

There are many areas of overseas operations which must be undertaken in such a manner that they comply fully with prevailing laws in the market.

Perhaps one of the things which will require special attention more than any other, is the appointment of overseas agents. A growing number of countries have strict laws on agency agreements, especially in respect of the termination of an agreement, and the obligation to pay agreed rates of commission. In addition, some countries have specific rules regarding the employment of personnel in an overseas agency.

In a similar manner a wide ranging list of legal requirements must be met if it is proposed to establish an overseas branch, manufacturing plant or assembly facility.

Another area which is fraught with legal minefields is the protection of trademarks. In many countries, for example Latin America, registration of trademarks is essential in order to establish any measure of protection. In addition it must be remembered that – in some jurisdictions – infringement of someone else's registration may be regarded as a criminal offence, with the possibility of a fine, or even jail and possibly seizure of goods. It is therefore of paramount importance to take the necessary steps to register trademarks in foreign countries.

Trademark laws vary from country to country, and the trademark position in each market must be assessed in each case. To some extent, even the definition of a trademark varies from country to country.

In the main a trademark is an identification tag which a manufacturer puts on his goods, to identify them from competitive products. A trademark can cover, for example, design marks such as the 'Esso' oval, as well as brand names such as 'Coca Cola', 'Kodak', or initials such as 'GM' or 'BP'. It may comprise an entire label or part of it, in fact any marking which helps the customer to tell one maker's product from another can be a trademark. To what extent a mark can be protected is often a legal conundrum and the answer will frequently vary from one jurisdiction to another.

As a general rule, words which merely describe the character or quality of goods are said to be descriptive and are thus not able to be protected. The theory being that everyone has a right to the normal use of language to describe his goods.

In some markets it is important to pay attention to religious beliefs or local superstitions. For example, in some countries the peacock is a bad luck symbol. In the same way a perfectly harmless English word may cause offence in some markets. It is therefore important to take local advice in order to establish whether a proposed trademark will have a local meaning preventing it from being used or protected as a trademark. It must be remembered that the indication that a trademark is registered may be a legal offence if marked goods are imported into a country where the mark is not registered.

In most major markets there are specialist organizations with detailed knowledge of prevailing trademark laws as, for example, in the United Kingdom the Chartered Institute of Trademark Agents.

Political stability

A matter of concern to all exporters is the political stability of overseas markets. Inevitably, with the overall growth of overseas markets, many new and potentially valuable markets become available each year.

For example, in recent years exporters have become increasingly aware of the enormous potential in South East Asia where countries are developing rapidly to provide a range of new export opportunities.

The risks arising from political instability are not new. An example of this is Cuba which before the second World War was an excellent market for British exporters. When Fidel Castro first came to power this created havoc for the exporters, due to embargoes placed on the acquisition of exchange to discharge overseas debts. This created a situation where many well established customers of British exporters, who had the necessary funds and were anxious to discharge their outstanding debts were unable to do so due to government imposed restrictions. Happily most of these debts were cleared eventually, but this involved lengthy delays.

An invaluable source of information on the political stability of overseas markets is the Department of Trade and Industry. The Department's country desk officers work closely with the Foreign and Commonwealth Office commercial staff overseas and can provide a wide range of information on individual markets, covering not only prospects for your products, with specific guidelines for doing business in a particular market, but also with special reference to the political and economic situation.

For many years the question of political stability has been a cause for concern in many markets in Latin America and also throughout Africa. All these areas can provide excellent export opportunities, but require special attention in assessing political stability. More recently the same problems have arisen in the Far East, an area of immense market potential for many British exporters.

In addition to the Department of Trade and Industry, reports on the political stability of various markets receive wide coverage in the media and it is recommended that such reports be studied and recorded in order to assess their implications for future marketing strategy.

Documentation

When undertaking overseas trade, one of the major differences compared with the home market is the need for specialized documentation which must be studied and understood.

An export shipment requires specific documents in order to meet the requirements of the importing country. Frequently the authorities in a foreign country will require specified documents, processed in a certain manner.

A major function of customs documents is to provide a complete and specific description of goods so that on arrival overseas they may be correctly assessed for duty purposes. In some instances documents may be required for the administration of exchange control regulations and for statistical purposes. It is most important that careful attention be given to every aspect of export documentation, first and foremost to ensure that goods can be cleared through customs without any problems or delay, also to avoid not only possible delays but also fines for incorrect documentation.

The documents most frequently required for export shipments

are: commercial invoice, consular invoice, certificate of origin, bill of lading.

In certain instances, the following may also be required: packing list, health certificate, import licence.

The commercial invoice is usually supplied on the exporter's own form, but the contents must comply with the requirements of the importing country. In some countries, especially members of the Commonwealth, the commercial invoices must be prepared on a special form prescribed by the customs authorities of the importing country. Such forms are usually obtainable from commercial stationers.

A consular invoice must be prepared with great care. It is most generally required in Latin America and certain other markets also require it. Basically a consular invoice calls for a detailed description of the goods together with details of marks, numbers, weights, value of goods and a declaration of origin and a declaration about the accuracy of the contents of the invoice. The forms are usually obtained from the consulate of the importing country, to whom the completed document must be submitted for legalization. A consular invoice is usually in the language of the importing country and must be completed in that language; it must not contain errors or alterations.

The main purpose of the certificate of origin is to establish the right of the goods to benefit from any preferential duties to which the importer might be entitled. In some markets consular verification of the certificate of origin is required or, alternatively, certification by a chamber of commerce.

A bill of lading or an air waybill is the key document in any export transaction. Legally, it is a receipt for goods received for shipment; it is in fact used as a document of title, and is regarded as a certificate of ownership which must be produced before delivery of the goods may be obtained. Many countries specify the number of copies, either negotiable or non-negotiable, of the bill of lading which must be supplied.

In addition to the basic essential elements of export documentation already mentioned, a number of markets have developed their own special documentation requirements as, for example, the documentation required for trade with the European Economic Community.

For more detail, it is recommended that reference be made to another book in this series entitled *International Physical Distribution;* this book deals in greater detail with a wide range of documentation problems.

Finance

An area of major difference when comparing British marketing and exporting is finance. In the home market a number of acceptable terms of payment are available, often being governed by the accepted practice in a given trade. For example, payment by monthly account is widely used.

However in the case of export transactions the exporter is faced with a very different problem. Obviously the most important aspect of any export transaction is to ensure that a secure method of payment is chosen: one which must be acceptable to the overseas customer, but which will also provide the maximum degree of security for the exporter.

Payment delays or bad debts can be costly and every effort must be made to prevent them. There are certain markets which are well-known as slow payers, and this is an area about which valuable information may be obtained from the major banks.

Obviously payment from overseas involves different procedures from those normally used in the home market. In many cases where problems arise it is because the exporter does not understand the special procedures, does not give appropriate instructions to the customer or in some cases fails to complete the necessary documentation correctly.

There are credit risks to be faced in any business transaction, but the exporter may face additional problems such as the imposition of exchange control and a variety of political or possibly war risks. In view of this an exporter would be wise to take credit insurance cover against these risks. Details of available options may be obtained from the Export Credits Guarantee Department.

Another option which may be considered is factoring. As mentioned in chapter one factoring services are available in both the home and export markets.

More detailed information on the finance of overseas trade will be found in another book in this series called *International Trade and Payments* by P. D. Briggs.

Overseas sales personnel

Perhaps the major difference between sales personnel in the home market and those operating overseas is the fact that export sales personnel must be able to operate efficiently without immediate supervision.

In the home market, it is a simple matter for sales personnel to have easy access to their sales manager in order to resolve any problems which may arise. However, in the case of overseas sales personnel, such a luxury is not available. They must be fully versed in the intricacies of export documentation and financial procedures, customs and transport facilities and will frequently be required to work at speed and under pressure, possibly in an unfamiliar environment.

Obviously, the need for speed, precision and the ability to withstand both physical and psychological pressures of the job also exist in the home market; they are significantly increased in international marketing.

A vital difference between home and overseas marketing is the level of responsibility and decision-making required by personnel engaged in marketing overseas. The personnel must have not only the ability but above all the authority to make management decisions. Nothing is more harmful to the prospects of concluding a transaction than when staff abroad feel that they have to ring head office for a decision. This is not well received by the customer.

Especially in the more advanced industrial markets, customers tend to be impatient and if the exporter is going to match the efforts of his competitors, it is vital that he or she have the ability and the authority to make major decisions on the spot.

Market segmentation

Market segmentation involves identifying areas of a market

which share common attributes, and can therefore be expected to respond in a similar manner to any marketing approach.

It is important to undertake a market segmentation exercise in any market. In the home market, depending of course on the product being marketed, there will be distinct segments each having its own special dislikes and varying degrees of disposable income. Indeed there will be examples of a product which may be much in demand in the South East, but could be quite unacceptable in the North East. It is important to identify these different segments of a market to enable a realistic sales plan to be produced.

Market segmentation is most important in overseas markets and the difference is one of degree. It must be appreciated that because of the sheer size of many overseas markets there will almost certainly be considerable differences in the way in which the different areas will respond to a marketing effort. An excellent example of a market where very great differences will be encountered is the United States. This is mainly due to the sheer size of the country. In addition factors such as climatic conditions and varying states of the economy will have a significant impact on the market.

The requirements in rural areas will be very different from those in highly industrialized areas. It is, therefore, very important to investigate and identify the many differences which arise in various segments of the market in order to enable sales and marketing plans to be devised to meet the varying needs. Indeed, in a market such as the United States, the size of the market and clearly defined regional differences will produce entirely different segments virtually amounting to totally different markets, all within the United States.

It will be easy to appreciate that there are significant problems to be faced in segmenting an overseas market, which will require a far greater effort than would be the case in the home market.

Overseas market research

In chapter 2, the principal aspects of market research were outlined. However it is necessary to stress the differences in undertaking market research in the home market and overseas markets.

The major advantage in the home market is the availability of a very extensive range of reliable secondary information. Here the key word is reliable, as for many overseas markets the available sources of information are limited and in some markets may well be unreliable.

There are a number of problems which may be encountered when undertaking market research overseas, which would not be encountered in the United Kingdom. Some of these differences are detailed below:

1 Due to cultural differences market research interviews may be difficult to obtain. In some markets interviews with females may not be possible.
2 A major problem in many markets will be the language barrier.
3 Spread and density of population may make both interviewing and sampling difficult.
4 In many markets reliable census information may not be available.
5 Poor communications may result in an unacceptably low response to postal surveys.
6 The interpretation of results may be suspect if carried out by someone of a different cultural background.

In any market, it is vital to undertake market research, not only before entering the market but on an ongoing basis. Although there are major differences in undertaking market research overseas, once an exporter is aware of the differences and problems, it is important that they be tackled and overcome.

Problems for the First Time Exporter

There are many important matters which must be considered by a newcomer to exporting.

It is important to undertake a careful study of the export selling price. Obviously it would be inappropriate to attempt to obtain export orders using prices which apply in the home market. Of major importance will be a study and consideration of competitors' prices in overseas markets. Above all it will be essential to make a thorough analysis of the additional costs involved in export trade, such as special packing requirements, freight charges, distribution costs, possible payment of agents' commission and duties payable overseas.

Market research must be undertaken to obtain a full understanding of the distribution systems in the overseas market, as these will probably be different from the situation in the home market.

A potential exporter must appreciate the problems involved in obtaining payment for its exports. According to the product and the particular market, all the available options must be considered in order to decide the steps to be taken to select a method of payment which will be acceptable to the overseas customer and above all provide the exporter with an assurance that payment will, in fact, be received. Unlike the normal open account method of payment in the home market, which of course may be appropriate for selected overseas customers, it may be decided to insist on payment by letter of credit, cash against documents or possibly the use of an intermediary such as an export house or an export merchant. Depending on the method chosen, especially for other methods of payment it will be necessary to consider the possible use of the Export Credit Guarantee Department (ECGD) or other credit insurance.

Agency Agreements

In chapter 6, details were given of the basic requirements which must be considered when selecting and appointing an overseas agent.

Very obviously this is a problem which does not arise in the home market. The conclusion of a satisfactory agency agreement with an appropriate candidate overseas will often be a major factor in building up a satisfactory export trade.

An important matter to be considered is that, in the main, an overseas agent will be representing the exporter, far away from home base and without the sort of day to day supervision which would be imposed on a home market representative.

Consequently an overseas agent must be regarded as a most important member of the marketing team who, in addition to the prime function of obtaining orders, will play a vital role in providing the exporter with frequent reports on the day to day economic and political situation in the market.

Such a representative will require comprehensive knowledge of both the products being offered in the market and of company policies and plans.

It has already been pointed out that, in the eyes of many customers, the agent will be thought of as 'the company' and consequently will bear far greater responsibilities to the company than would his counterpart in the home market.

Questions for Discussion

1 What do you understand by the term 'market segmentation'?

2 Describe the documents most frequently required for export shipments.

3 How would you undertake market research in an overseas market?

Marketing in Practice

The Decision to Export

From the earlier chapters it will be appreciated that marketing is a complex function, embracing the use of a variety of disciplines, all of which must be understood and coordinated to achieve a successful marketing operation.

A decision to export must in no way be regarded as an ancillary activity, designed to find an outlet for surplus production or goods for which there is no longer a demand in the home market.

Exporting is a vital and integral part of a company's marketing strategy for which there must be an acceptance of the need to make a suitable investment, not only in financial terms but also in time and personnel. A marketing plan must take into consideration the following factors.

1 The present and potential size of the targeted market, based on the results of a market research exercise.
2 A comprehensive study of the competition, both from other exporters and from domestic production in the target market.
3 A detailed study of prices in the market, including the additional costs to be met in an export operation.
4 An estimate of the expenditure which will have to be made in order to provide the necessary advertising, promotion and servicing support for the product.

5 An evaluation of any product modifications which may be necessary to meet the needs of the market.
6 A comprehensive study of both the tariff and non-tariff barriers to trade which must be overcome.
7 An investigation of the possible methods of transport and distribution.
8 Establishment of both short and long term sales and profit targets.
9 A comprehensive assessment of the financial implications of the foregoing, together with an assessment of any possible political or credit risks.

International Distribution

A vital aspect of export practice is the establishment of an efficient system of distribution. In order to achieve this the specialist export staff responsible for distribution arrangements must be trained and qualified for the job.

In order to understand the major factors involved in international distribution, it is necessary to consider the following elements involved in the processing of an export consignment, and to be aware of the need to keep a close check on costs and to seek the most appropriate arrangements for each consignment.

1 An adequate and clear description of the goods being exported.
2 Full specification of the goods, using, where appropriate, the metric system.
3 Precise details of the quantities involved, together with details of delivery times required.
4 Comprehensive price details, showing amounts per unit, currency and delivery terms, such as FOB and CIF.
5 Terms of payment.
6 Terms of delivery, such as: ex-stock, forward, and others.
7 Details of modes of transport, such as: road haulage, containers, air freight.
8 Insurance details.

9 Packaging and packing.
10 Offer by pro-forma invoice.
11 Miscellaneous including: identity of goods and country of origin.

Essentially export marketing involves satisfying a demand which may be consumer or industry oriented. To ensure success, a wide range of factors must be taken into account, especially the following.

■ Care must be taken in fixing the correct selling price in order to achieve market penetration and adequate sales volume.
■ Successful exporting does not just result from trying to find a market for products which may be available. The object of the exercise is to offer products which have been produced to meet the specific needs of the market. A customer profile on the type of product required, in terms of price, colour, size, performance and design will be established by market research.
■ Every care must be taken to establish, possibly with help from Technical Help for Exporters, which safety and technical standards will be required in the market.
■ Initial research will be required to establish the degree of competition to be overcome. It is possible that one or two established brands in the market present competition which must be overcome by offering a technically superior product or possibly providing superior distribution and after-sales service.
■ In certain markets it may be necessary to overcome rules and regulations regarding such matters as promotion, distribution and retailing methods. In some cases imports must be made through a government agency which operates an import quota system, in order to control the volume of imports and protect domestic producers. Important information on these matters should be obtained by consulting the Department of Trade and Industry. The information available from this source will enable a decision to be made as to whether or not it is worthwhile trying to enter the market. Before attempting to promote products overseas

careful attention must be paid to all available market reports and market research findings.

- Consideration must be given to possible currency fluctuations taking, where possible, adequate safeguards.
- The precise terms of an export sales contract must be clearly defined, and where possible adequate safeguards should be built into the contract.
- Precise terms of delivery have been established by the International Chamber of Commerce. The most commonly used terms are listed in Incoterms 1990, details of which are given in chapter 6.

Creating a Marketing and Sales Plan

In order to succeed in marketing overseas it is essential to devise an effective marketing and sales plan. This must define clearly what it is hoped to achieve in a market, and explain how these aims will be attained.

The plan will normally be devised by the export marketing manager; it must be discussed with and agreed by everyone who will be involved in its execution, as it will form part of a company's overall sales and marketing plans and hence cannot be considered in isolation from the company's other activities. Despite the importance of export trade, it should be appreciated that this represents but one facet of the company's overall operations. Essentially the plan is a blueprint of the action and techniques which will be implemented to secure successful business overseas.

The marketing and sales plan will vary from one company to another, bearing in mind the variety of products and markets which may be covered. Some of the basic essentials to be incorporated in a plan are detailed below.

1 Clearly defined marketing objectives which may be established by product, country or region.
2 A budgeted sales income, again by product, country or region.
3 The time-scale to achieve the marketing objectives, making sure that provision is made to allow adequate lead time.

4 A detailed analysis of available selling resources. This must consider the available options of direct sales, selling through an intermediary or through overseas agents.

5 Proposals for ways in which the product will be promoted. The choice will be governed by both the product and the cost of any promotion, which would include brochures, catalogues, trade fairs, sponsorships, television and press advertising.

6 Distribution plans, to be determined by the export sales terms, and may involve the use of the services of a freight forwarder.

7 Details of credit control arrangements to ensure that the all important payment is received.

8 A market analysis, covering market trends, market shares, and projected profit margins.

9 Finally the plan should indicate the prospects for future developments.

A vital ingredient of marketing is the establishment of an efficient distribution system to enable marketing plans to be achieved.

It must be stressed that delays in deliveries or damage of goods in transit will have a disastrous effect on future sales prospects, as will, for example, incorrect documentation or poor after-sales service.

An example of a company which had great success, not only in producing a good product, but in appreciating and capitalizing on market trends is Hoover. Murray Spangler, who was employed as a caretaker in an apartment block in North Canton, Ohio, USA, who's duties included sweeping carpets, devised a machine to suck dust out of the carpets and blow it into a bag. In 1907 he showed a model of his electric suction sweeper to a relative, William Hoover, who was a local harness and leather goods manufacturer.

Unknown to either of them, an English civil engineer, Hubert Cecil Booth, had invented a similar machine in England in 1901. Booth's domestic vacuum cleaner was heavy and hard to use. Spangler's machine was lighter and far easier to push. Hoover immediately saw the potential of Spangler's model and bought the manufacturing rights.

In 1908 Hoover began to manufacture the cleaner. It ran on

wheels and had a dust bag attached to a long handle. It was an immediate success and within ten years Hoover's company stopped manufacturing leather goods and concentrated on vacuum cleaners. In 1909 the company adopted the slogan 'It beats as it sweeps as it cleans' and set up an office in London to sell cleaners shipped from a Canadian factory. In 1932 the first British factory was opened at Perivale in Middlesex. In 1948 washing machines were added to the range.

The British arm of the company now manufactures more than one million vacuum cleaners and half a million washing machines a year. In addition to the overall growth of the company and the sales achievements in Britain, a further measure of the successful penetration of a market, with effective promotion of the product is the fact that the company's name has now become part of the English language. The Collins English Dictionary contains the following definition. Hoover – trademark, a type of vacuum cleaner. Verb, to vacuum clean a carpet, furniture etc.

Overseas Marketing Channels

In comparison with the home market, there are many more possible channels of distribution to be investigated and evaluated in markets overseas, as explained in chapter 1.

In its simplest form marketing is the function which aims to satisfy a demand for goods, at a profit. The enormous cost of setting up a production line requires a manufacturer to have an accurate assessment of the potential market and available channels of distribution before embarking on production.

When considering available options it is always important to consider the existing methods of distribution and to determine if these can be improved upon.

An important factor in developing new marketing channels is to consider not only direct export, or exporting through an intermediary, but also to consider overseas assembly or production.

Marketing communications, such as advertising, sales promotion and publicity provide a wide range of opportunities to establish new marketing channels.

In order to succeed in marketing overseas, all the above factors must be explored and developed. Nevertheless the most important element in a successful marketing campaign is the presentation of a quality product which has its own special features and is capable of meeting any possible competition.

A good example of a first class product which was successfully promoted and sold all over the world is the Morris 1000.

After the second World War, the Nuffield organization produced the first Morris Minor. This car was designed by Alec Issigonis who in later years designed the highly successful Mini, which still continues to be a very popular small car.

In 1945 the British government coined the phrase 'Export or die' and made every possible effort to ensure that scarce materials were made available to companies who had products with export potential. The Morris Minor was introduced at the Earls Court motor show in London in October 1948 and was an instant success.

Due to its quality and unique features as a successful small family car, supported by first class promotion and advertising, within the first three years the company was exporting over 80 per cent of production, such was the success of the product and the marketing operation. The car was very well received in the United States the only problem being its low performance with a top speed of sixty miles per hour.

The car was marketed successfully all over the world, and by 1950 the one hundred thousandth car was exported.

In November 1951 Morris cars merged with Austin to form the British Motor Corporation, and in 1956 a new 948cc engine was produced to create the Morris 1000, with greatly enhanced performance.

By December 1960 it became the first British car to achieve sales of over one million units.

The last Morris 1000 was made in 1970, but due to the excellence of the product and the successful marketing on a worldwide basis it did not die. In fact, it is estimated that one hundred thousand examples are still in daily use around the world today.

Market Penetration

As explained in chapter 4, participation in overseas trade fairs provides an excellent opportunity to promote products in overseas markets, and may often be the first step in establishing a worldwide marketing operation. It should not be thought that overseas trade fairs are a recent innovation. They have for many years enabled a number of companies to develop their activities in a number of markets, as illustrated by the following example.

In 1867 the Reverend Edward Johns made a timely investment when he bought the sanitary pottery which had been operating for some fifty years in the Staffordshire village of Armitage. Sanitation was very much a topic of the day at that time, and the death of Prince Albert from typhoid in 1861 concentrated the public's mind on hygiene. Demand for the new sanitary ware, first patented in the 1840s, grew rapidly and Reverend Johns was soon in competition with another pioneer in the business, a Scottish plumber called John Shanks who founded his company in Paisley in 1851.

Edward Johns did much to establish British manufacturers in the world's export markets. In 1876 Armitage products were exhibited at the Philadelphia exhibition in the United States. The company achieved extensive sales in the States and also a measure of renown by the adoption of the term 'John' for the water closet. In a similar manner in India and China a water closet is referred to as a 'Shanko'.

Resold in 1900, the Staffordshire factory continued to trade as Edward Johns until 1960, when it adopted the name by which its products had long been known, Armitage Ware. A number of significant developments were made to improve the product and meet customers' demands. Initially sanitary ware had been white, although some firms produced elaborate decorations. However to meet changing tastes and customer demand, Armitage introduced the first mass-produced coloured sanitary ware.

In 1969 Armitage merged with Shanks and the group is now the largest sanitary ware manufacturer in Britain, employing more than three thousand people.

From the initial penetration of a major export market in 1876 when Armitage ware was shown at the Philadelphia exhibition, factories in the United Kingdom and around the world now export to some ninety countries. From the original humble beginnings, products now range from highly specialized fittings for use in submarines to the most luxurious bathroom equipment in a host of colours and designs.

Export Correspondence

In spite of the introduction of modern technology to speed and improve worldwide communications, export correspondence still provides a vital role in both establishing and maintaining contacts with customers overseas. It frequently happens that for long periods letters will provide the principal means of contact between an exporter and his foreign buyers or agents. Appreciating how to carry out export correspondence is an aspect of export expertise which is frequently neglected. It is easy to assume that export correspondence is just like any other, governed by only basic rules: be prompt, be precise and be polite.

One of the first problems to consider is the language which should be used. Possibly the least satisfactory solution is to write in English and ask for replies in English, with the obvious exception of English speaking markets. Correspondence in the appropriate foreign language will do much to establish goodwill and confidence with overseas customers and agents. However, as previously mentioned with reference to advertising and publicity, it is vital to ensure that the translation of material is accurate and correct.

An important factor is the overall appearance of a letter, indeed one of the first essentials for an exporter is a well designed and produced letterhead. Always remember that a letter may well be the overseas customer's first contact with the exporter, and first impressions are most important. The letterhead must give all the necessary information, the company's name, address (do not forget to include England), telephone and fax numbers and cable address, telex number.

One of the most important rules of export correspondence is

to deal with all correspondence promptly. If, for example, an exporter receives an enquiry for a product which is not available immediately, do not just file the letter and forget about it. This would amount to very poor and possibly damaging public relations. A brief well written letter explaining the situation and promising to contact the writer of the letter as soon as the situation changes will give the overseas enquirer a much more favourable impression.

In a similar manner promptness is essential when acknowledging an order, especially when it will take time to produce and dispatch it. If possible give your overseas customer an approximate date of dispatch, with an estimated time of arrival. If there is any need to settle shipping arrangements, the necessary correspondence should be initiated at once. Any shipping delays should be explained with suitable apologies.

It must be said that letters do have some limitations. In a highly competitive export market, mail may be too slow in certain circumstances. Today, telephone, telex, fax, cable and on-line links may be essential to take care of urgent matters.

Never forget that these options anticipate or supplement letters but do not replace them altogether. Telephone conversations should be confirmed by letter, and letters can amplify the basic details in a cable or telex.

Another important aspect of foreign correspondence is persistence. It often happens that a number of letters will accomplish what one may fail to do. Ongoing correspondence is vitally important, not only to initiate, but above all to stimulate the interests of overseas customers and agents. It is important for an overseas agent to be regarded as a vital member of the marketing team.

He should be constantly updated on any new products which are being developed, also any possible supply problems which may be foreseen, together with reports on general trends in the industry. In a similar manner an exporter will hope to receive a regular flow of correspondence from overseas agents, not only maintaining contact but above all supplying market reports and intelligence.

Persistence also means following up contacts, opportunities, or sales initiatives. On returning from an overseas trip or trade fair it will often be productive to write to all the companies and individuals who have been contacted, in the hope of ensuring profitable future dealings in the market.

Barriers to International Trade

In chapters 8 and 9, mention was made of some of the non-tariff barriers which may be encountered, together with suggestions for possible ways of overcoming some of these barriers. There is always a danger that markets impose sanctions against an exporting country.

A recent example is a long standing dispute between the United States and the European Community with reference to electrical generating equipment and the field of telecommunications.

Early in 1993 the Community resolved to remove restrictions on American companies competing with European manufacturers in the lucrative market for electrical generating equipment. However, at that time the Community did not agree to remove similar restriction in the telecommunications field. In the light of failure to reach agreement on this trade dispute involving government contracts, the United States decided to impose partial trade sanctions against the Community.

In the above example the economic impact of these particular sanctions would be minimal, however it was admitted on both sides that the fear would be that any such trade restrictions could easily spark off the tit-for-tat trade war of retaliation, which in turn could so easily jeopardize a much sought General Agreement on Tariffs and Trade accord on global trade liberalization.

Internationalization

Since the early 1980s there has been a significant increase in the internationalization of business.

In order to understand this trend it is necessary to consider what may motivate a company to make investments in overseas markets. There are many reasons for making such decisions of which the following are examples:

- To take advantage of lower labour costs in a market and thereby increase profitability.
- To locate production facilities in a market which has an available pool of skilled labour.
- To locate production facilities closer to target markets and thereby eliminate expensive freight charges.
- To establish a base in a country and gain a ready means of access to a nearby trading bloc.

In the United Kingdom many American and Japanese companies have invested in new production facilities, taking advantage of available skilled labour and providing an entrée for trade within the European Community. An example of this strategy was the Japanese Nissan Car Company who made a large investment in their factory in the United Kingdom, and introduced both high-tech production facilities and also new management practices. This investment has been highly successful, with increasing productivity and an absence of labour problems.

A similar investment was made by another Japanese car manufacturer with the establishment of a new Honda factory in Swindon.

Perhaps one of the most dramatic moves was the one made by the Honda company in 1988. At that time, the Rover car company was in the doldrums, but a strategic deal was reached with the Honda company. Rover got the best in Japanese technology in return for an interest in the Rover company; of major importance was the fact that the deal involved Rover in embracing Japanese industrial philosophy. An example is that the word 'worker' was abolished, and everyone became an associate. Similarly, from the plant's director down everyone wears corporate workwear. From the dereliction of a sprawling British Leyland plant, an entirely new factory, with a large element of robot operations was built. This new factory combines the best of two philosophies. On the one hand the Cowley-styled body of the latest model, the Rover 600 with it's Viking longboat grille badge, walnut door cappings and stainless steel styling accents exudes a comfortable Englishness; engines, gearboxes and running gear are shipped in from Japan.

Honda also builds a similar vehicle, the Accord at the new Swindon factory.

In addition to such investments in Britain, a growing number of manufacturers have recently made large investments in the Far East. The reasons for these moves are two fold. Not only are these markets able to offer a ready source of low cost labour, helping to reduce production costs, but a further advantage is the creation of production facilities which are close to the rapidly growing Far East markets.

Japanese car manufacturers have established production facilities in Malaysia for example, as have a number of well-known European manufacturers such as Bosch, the German manufacturer of electrical equipment.

The Far East not only provides a vast potential market for both industrial and consumer goods, but also welcomes overseas investments which provide an opportunity to develop their own economies.

China is a truly vast country which is anxious to improve its economy and to develop modern production facilities. In the early 1990s the Ford motor company plan to commence production of car parts in China following agreement for a $90m joint venture with the Shanghai Automotive Industry Corporation. In addition the two companies plan a $500m joint venture, to research fuel systems, air conditioning and glass.

Another example of the growth of internationalization is the decision by Japan's three major aircraft makers to join Boeing and Europe's Airbus Industries in a study looking at the feasibility of super-jumbo jets. The new aircraft which would be capable of carrying 600 to 800 passengers could be twice the size of the major workhorse of the world's airlines, the Boeing 747–400 and be ready for service by the year 2002.

A matter of major concern for companies contemplating making investment overseas is the possibility of restrictions on the repatriation of profits. In the early days of overseas investment projects some countries limited the amount of earnings which could be taken out of the country. However, many developing countries, wishing to attract overseas investments and the acquisition of expertise now appreciate that such a strategy discourages investments by foreign companies.

An example of the changing situation is Bangladesh, a country which had restrictions on foreign exchange and had rules which limited the amount of surplus earnings which foreign companies could take out of the country. The rules were changed in 1993 allowing foreign companies to remit all their surpluses, and also making it possible for foreign companies to borrow local currency without limit.

With the creation of the Single European Market, there are incentives not only for European companies to invest in Britain, but also for British companies to invest in Europe. An example of this is Boots the Chemists, the Nottingham based company whose over the counter medicine and consumer products division strengthened its European operations with the takeover of a French and an Italian healthcare business at a cost of £14.5m, in line with its strategy of boosting healthcare brands in Europe.

Another example of the changing pattern of international trade is the return of American business to Vietnam. In April 1993 an American consulting firm opened for business in Hanoi, being the first American company to operate officially in Vietnam since the end of the war in 1975. The Vietnam American Trade and Investment Consulting Company will advise other firms interested in penetrating Vietnam's market of seventy million people.

In addition to overseas investments, the growth of internationalization also provides many new opportunities for employment overseas, in countries which are anxious to develop a range of home-based industries.

Early in 1993 a survey was published by management consultants Price Waterhouse; this reached the conclusion that, due to the increasing internationalization of business, growing numbers of employees could expect to be offered some form of employment abroad during their career.

It should be emphasized that internationalization has, in fact, existed for many years, although the time of maximum growth in this field commenced in the early 1980s.

An early example of international cooperation in the field of manufacturing and marketing is the Nestlé company. A Swiss research chemist Henri Nestlé developed a milk food for babies which was a great success. The product was first introduced in 1867 at a time when one Swiss baby in five died before its first birthday. Initially the product was distributed through the medical profession. By 1873 the Nestlé plant at Vevey on the shores of Lake Geneva was producing half a million cans a year.

At the same time a confectioner in Vevey, Daniel Peter, collaborated with Henri Nestlé to produce the world's first milk chocolate. Eventually the Daniel Peter business was taken over by Nestlé.

At this time, a hundred miles to the North East of Vevey another dairy enterprise had also been launched in 1867. This was a condensed milk plant built by Charles Page, an American, in Zurich. Page had realized the potential of preserved milk, made by evaporation using a process which his compatriot Bail Borden had patented in 1856. His decision to launch the operation in Switzerland was influenced by the fact that Switzerland at that time had a population of only two million people but had one million cows. Page looked upon the United Kingdom as a potential market, and with this in mind called his business the Anglo-Swiss Condensed Milk Company.

In 1877 Anglo-Swiss introduced a milk food in direct competition with Nestlé, and in the following year Nestlé responded by going into condensed milk production.

Because of the success of their products, both companies flourished and grew rapidly. By this time the Anglo-Swiss Condensed Milk Company had expanded its operations establishing condenseries not only throughout Europe, but also in the United States.

In 1875 Henri Nestlé sold his company to a group in Geneva, which retained the company name which had by now established a reputation throughout the world.

In 1905 the two companies merged, retaining the name Nestlé and remaining a Swiss company. Further product developments followed and in 1938 Nescafé, the first instant coffee was launched.

Today Nestlé claims to be the largest food company in the world, with interests in virtually every nation. In addition to dairy, chocolate and coffee products the company also manufactures major brands of frozen, canned and packeted foods, including in Britain such brands as Findus, Libby's and Chambourcy.

Dun and Bradstreet in London publish a range of directories entitled *Who Owns Whom*, which give details of the many mergers and takeovers which have taken place over a number of years, as a result of ever-growing internationalization.

Questions for Discussion

1 Describe marketing channels which might be considered for an overseas market.

2 What are the essential factors to be considered when undertaking export correspondence?

3 What do you understand by the term 'internationalization'? Give two examples.

Recommended Reading

The following books in this series are expected to be published by Blackwell Publishers in 1994.

KOULADIS, N., *Principles of Law Relating to International Trade*.
BRIGGS, P. D., *Principles of International Trade and Payments*.
SHERLOCK, J., *Principles of International Physical Distribution*.
SPENCER, J., *Principles of International Marketing*.
GROVES, L. W. J., *Principles of International Market Research*.
CONLAN, J., *Principles of Management in Export*.

Other Publications

WALSH, L. S., *International Marketing*, McDonald & Evans, 1981.
GILLINGAN, Colin and HERD, Martin, *International Marketing*, Croom Helm, 1986.
Export Today (Official Journal of the Institute of Export).
Journal of the Institute of Freight Forwarders.
INSTEP (Quarterly newsletter of the British Standards Institute)
International Trade Forum (publication of International Trade Centre/UNCTAD/GATT).
International Freighting Weekly.
Journal of Commerce.
SITPRO News Bulletin.
Lloyds List and Shipping Gazette.

Export Times.
Incoterms 1990, International Chamber of Commerce, 38 Cours Albert 1er, 7508 Paris, France.
Technical Help for Exporters (THE) brochures, BSI Standards, Lingford Wood, Milton Keynes, MK14 6LE.

Department of Trade and Industry publications. The Department of Trade and Industry offers an extensive range of invaluable publications. Full details appear in a catalogue, available free of charge from DTI Library and Information Centre, Room 101, Ashdown House, 123 Victoria Street, London SW1E 6RB or from the Department's nearest regional office.

Other Sources of Information

- International divisions of major banks: Barclays, Midland, National Westminster and Lloyds. All these major banks produce valuable free booklets covering aspects of marketing overseas.
- Chambers of Commerce
- Export Clubs
- Local branches of The Institute of Export
- Local branches of The Institute of Freight Forwarders
- Trade Associations
- Confederation of British Industries
- Export Credits Guarantee Department
- Foreign Embassies
- Foreign Information Bureaux in the United Kingdom
- The Statistics Office of the European Community

Glossary

Dumping (usually used in the phrase **anti-dumping**) The sale abroad of goods at below cost price in order to wipe out competition.

Factor A finance company or bank which takes over debts on exports in exchange for a percentage fee.

Incoterms The list of phrases and their initials devised by the International Chamber of Commerce to identify internationally the stage in the delivery of export goods to which the quotation refers (for example, EXW = ex-works or FOB = Free on Board).

Marketing mix A selection of activities designed to make a product acceptable in a market.

Product mix A selection of products that a company decides to sell into a particular market.

Index

agency agreements, 85-9
agents,
    commission, 83
    del credere, 68
American National Standards Institute (ANSI), 127
Association of British Chambers of Commerce, 25
barter, 79
British Overseas Trade Board (BOTB), 20
British Standards Institution (BSI), 126
buyback, 79
buying offices, 8
Canadian Standards Association (CSA), 127
Central Office of Information (COI), 47
concessionaires, 77
Confederation of British Industry (CBI), 24
confirming house, 74-5
consortia, 77
countertrade, 79
Department of Trade and Industry (DTI), 52, 53, 110-11
Escrow Trading Account, 80
European Committees for Standardization (CEN, CENELEC), 23,
    128
Export Credits Guarantee Department (ECGD), 67
Export Data Services, 22
Export House, 7

Export Market Information Centre, 22
Export Marketing Research Scheme (EMRS), 19, 24-5
export merchant, 7, 73
Export Today, 24
factoring, 8, 68
franchising 78-9
General Agreement on Tariffs and Trade (GATT), 116-17
Incoterms, 72
International Airlines Transport Association (IATA), 113
International Electrotechnical Commission (IEC), 127
inward missions, 81, 101
International News on Standards and Exporting (INSTEP), 130
joint ventures, 52
licensing, 78
Market Information Enquiry Service (MIES), 20, 64
offset trading, 80
outward missions, 81
Overseas Promotion Support Branch (OPS), 81
overseas sales representatives, 81-2
Overseas Status Report Service (OSRS), 67
product mix, 8-10
Projects and Export Policy Division (PEP), 82
Switch Trading, 80
Technical Help for Exporters (THE), 23-4, 126, 129-30
test marketing, 37
turnkey operation, 123